TraderMind

TraderMind

Get a Mindful Edge in the Markets

*How to Train Your Mind,
Manage Your Emotions,
Enhance Your Decisions and
Maximise Your Profits*

Steve Ward

WILEY

This edition first published 2015
© 2015 Steve Ward

Registered office
John Wiley & Sons Ltd, The Atrium, Southern Gate, Chichester,
West Sussex, PO19 8SQ, United Kingdom

For details of our global editorial offices, for customer services and for information about how to apply for permission to reuse the copyright material in this book please see our website at www.wiley.com.

Wiley publishes in a variety of print and electronic formats and by print-on-demand. Some material included with standard print versions of this book may not be included in e-books or in print-on-demand. If this book refers to media such as a CD or DVD that is not included in the version you purchased, you may download this material at http://booksupport.wiley.com. For more information about Wiley products, visit www.wiley.com.

Designations used by companies to distinguish their products are often claimed as trademarks. All brand names and product names used in this book are trade names, service marks, trademarks or registered trademarks of their respective owners. The publisher is not associated with any product or vendor mentioned in this book.

Limit of Liability/Disclaimer of Warranty: While the publisher and author have used their best efforts in preparing this book, they make no representations or warranties with respect to the accuracy or completeness of the contents of this book and specifically disclaim any implied warranties of merchantability or fitness for a particular purpose. It is sold on the understanding that the publisher is not engaged in rendering professional services and neither the publisher nor the author shall be liable for damages arising herefrom. If professional advice or other expert assistance is required, the services of a competent professional should be sought.

Library of Congress Cataloging-in-Publication Data
Ward, Steve, 1969-
 Tradermind : get a mindful edge in the markets / Steve Ward.
   pages cm
 Includes bibliographical references and index.
 ISBN 978-1-118-31854-6 (paperback)
 1. Investments—Psychological aspects. 2. Speculation—Psychological aspects. I. Title.
 HG4515.15.W368 2014
 332.601'9—dc23
                                                                2014028284

A catalogue record for this book is available from the British Library.

ISBN 9781118318546 (paperback)
ISBN 9781118316733 (ebk)
ISBN 9781118316740 (ebk)
ISBN 9781118994924 (ebk)

Cover Design: Wiley

Cover Illustration: ©Shutterstock.com/Roman Ya

Set in 10/14 pt Meridien LT Std by Aptara Inc., New Delhi, India

Printed in the UK

To Sabine, Oliver and Casper
Mum, Dad and Debs
"Team Ward"

Contents

About the Author

Steve Ward has over 20 years of teaching, training and coaching experience, having started out working in sports and performance psychology with elite athletes and teams in over 30 different sports and with high performers in the corporate sector.

Since 2005 he has focused on working with traders and fund managers from investment banks, hedge funds, energy companies, asset management funds, leading proprietary trading groups and with independent traders across the globe. He utilises a unique blend of performance psychology, neuroscience, behavioural finance, mindfulness-based approaches and neuropsychology coaching in his work, with a focus on providing practical techniques and strategies.

Steve is the author of *High Performance Trading: 35 Practical Strategies To Enhance Your Trading Psychology and Performance*, was the consultant trading performance coach to BBC TV's *Million Dollar Traders* series, co-managed a team of 45 professional proprietary traders in London and has written for many leading trading publications. He has also traded stock indices and FX on his own account and is a member of the Association for Coaching, Association of Contextual Behavioural Science, Society for Neuroeconomics, Association of NeuroPsychoEconomics and Society for Neuroscience.

Performance Edge Consulting Ltd

Performance Edge Consulting Ltd is a trading psychology and performance consultancy which offers specialist coaching and training services to banks, hedge funds, energy companies, proprietary trading groups, asset management funds, independent traders, brokerages, exchanges and trading education providers. Find out more at www.performanceedgeconsulting.co.uk.

Foreword

When Steve Ward wrote his first book 6 years ago on High Performance Trading, (packed with practical strategies), I thought he had covered all bases! I have known Steve for a number of years and wondered what more he could possibly add. Steve is a gifted communicator and powerfully intuitive coach. This has attracted some of the world's most outstanding traders and fund managers as clients. You see, it does not matter how much experience or success one has had in the business of trading the markets, everyone can use objective feedback or coaching to keep concentration levels up and performance on track. Challenges have increased with an expanding amount of information, stimulus and distractions. Steve once again has delivered a compelling book that combines a thoughtful read with "bang-for-the buck" practical strategies for time pressed traders. In fact, the more experience you have the more you will appreciate this gem of a book.

Four counterintuitive points jumped out at me that illustrate a different way of thinking about things that Steve brings to light.

A common cliché newer traders hear is, "trade your plan" along with the need for "discipline". Steve reframes our thinking with the concept of "impermanence". Winning and losing runs are impermanent. Changes in the market are impermanent. Thus, "rigidly sticking to your trading plan once the conditions have changed...is like a sports team sticking to a game plan that is not working". Holding on to the idea of impermanence can help you be more flexible. Steve's focus is to develop your mindset to make decisions that reflect the current market environment...which is always changing. Awareness...flexibility...discipline...three overlapping yet independent issues.

Another interesting point that Steve has researched is why smart people can underperform. The crux of this comes from the environment we are in – one charged with high amounts of information and sensory overload. Too much stimulation results in distractibility and impatience. Steve offers some short and practical tactics through mindfulness exercises to re-center and focus. The positive emotions experienced as a result of these simple tricks are a great tool for combating this "Attention Deficit Trait".

Steve offers a whole section on the trading difficulties and challenges that even the industry's star traders encounter: extended losing runs, changes in market conditions, stressful life events.... Not only will his tools help you develop the resilience required to deal with these events, but he also provides a satisfying answer as to why emotions can still be attached to an event and thus how to free oneself in order to move on. "How can I get rid of the memory of the big loss I took earlier this year?"...! The cost of this book is a small price to pay to learn the answer to that common question (!)

Lastly, a most wonderful but yet another counterintuitive reframing: Emotions! How many times have traders been told that emotions are bad, emotions get in the way of trading, successful traders are less emotional.... yet Steve explains how emotions are essential to the decision making process and how they keep our brains focused on critical information. Emotional factors in decision making can serve a purpose. In classic "Steve Ward" fashion, he grounds his guidance in solid neuroscience research and scientific explanations.

Only a masterful communicator and coach can additionally present an 8-week mindfulness training program in just five pages at the end. Home Run!

Linda Raschke
LBRGroup, Inc., CTA
Chicago, Illinois

Acknowledgements

The visible results of any individual performer are often an outcome that is enabled through a more invisible support team. In my case, as author of this book, the people in that team are numerous and I would like to take this opportunity to thank them for the contributions they have made and for the support they have provided in enabling me to produce this book.

Firstly, a huge thank you to the core members of "Team Ward", my beautiful wife Sabine and my two amazing sons Oliver and Casper for their love and support through what must have seemed like the writing of the longest book ever.

Secondly, to Linda Raschke (www.lindaraschke.net) for the time she has given both in providing her expertise and experience in the form of feedback during the writing progress, and then for going above and beyond the call of duty by agreeing to write the foreword to this book.

Thirdly, to all the traders and people involved in the institutions I work with, who provide me with the opportunity to utilise my skills and expertise but who also teach me a great many things, and whose interactions enable me to get the rich insights that I am able to share with the readers of this book.

Fourthly, to the people who have been the front runners in moving areas such as neuroscience and mindfulness-based approaches to the fore, the developers, researchers, authors and trainers who have influenced my work over the years and whose outstanding work this book is built upon.

Finally, to the team at Wiley whose support, expertise and most importantly extreme patience have encouraged and enabled me to move from an idea through to this finished book... *TraderMind*.

Introduction: The Evolution of *TraderMind*

The Challenges of Trading and Investing

Trading and investing performance occurs at the point where the trader and the market meet, where decisions are made and P&L (profit and loss) is ultimately won or lost. Traders and fund managers must take risk under conditions of uncertainty and be able to manage the outcomes of those decisions and their consequences, as well as coping with the wider pressures and stresses that trading can bring. This is a psychologically challenging environment. Humans favour certainty over uncertainty, and when you take financial risk in such an ambiguous environment, with imperfect information and with high consequences, you are influenced (largely outside your awareness) by a whole number of brain, mind and even body processes that can influence your decision making and behaviour in ways that lead to market returns which are sub-optimal. Emotions, your mood, your thoughts, beliefs and perceptions, your attention, mental shortcuts, your energy levels, the environment you are in, your past and recent performance, your hormones and your patterns and habits of behaviour are all factors that can play a part in your trading and investing decisions.

Furthermore, changes in market conditions, increased competition in the markets, regulatory changes, institutional restructuring, growing automation and the rise of high-frequency trading, information overload and increasing pressures to perform have exacerbated the demands placed on traders and fund managers over recent years.

Trader meets market.

Beyond Skills and Strategy

Karl is a commodities trader who trades predominantly intraday with some overnights being held where required. Over the last few months he has been trying to run his trades a little further. He has a good belief in the levels that he selects in the markets, and his performance over the last few months has been relatively stable despite some choppy market conditions. When we meet he is keen to look at ways to hold his trades for longer. His profit targets are typically around ten ticks (price movements) and yet he is more often than not getting out at around three ticks as a reaction to noise in the market, or his position moving offside (against him), only to see on many occasions that his original target level eventually gets hit. He knows what he wants to achieve from his trades, and believes in his ability to pick good levels at which to enter and exit the market, yet more often than not he doesn't follow through with his plans.

Take a moment to reflect on your own trading and investing experience. Have you ever:

- Taken profits too early, before your profit level was hit?
- Run losses too far or moved your stop further away to avoid a loss?
- Taken trades that were not part of your strategy or approach?
- Not taken trades that were part of your strategy or approach?
- Taken too much risk; traded too big?
- Taken too little risk; traded too small?
- Chased your losses, or revenge traded?
- Overtraded in a state of euphoria?
- Traded through boredom?

All of these – as I can testify from my experience in working with thousands of traders and fund managers across the globe and across asset classes – are quite common trading behaviours.

As early as 1759 in *The Theory of Moral Sentiments*,[1] Adam Smith described the battle between the *"impartial spectator"* and the *"passions"*, between knowing what is right and best and the challenge of temptation and instant gratification. Not much has changed in all those years – Warren Buffett talks in a similar way about traders and investors needing to avoid the *"temptations and urges"* that get other traders into trouble. We are still fitted with the same mental software, the same brain information-processing systems, and as a result we are still experiencing the same dilemma. The key challenge in trading is not so much "Knowing What To Do" (KWTD) as "Doing What You Know" (DWYK). This creates the psychological gap that exists between having a strategy with a positive expectancy and actually trading it in such a way that it returns something close to those expected profits. One very experienced trader I worked with in a training session at a leading investment bank remarked how just being able to get better at running his profits and cutting his losses would have a considerable impact on his P&L, and how this was true for other traders in his team and across the trading floor.

To perform well in the markets you need more than just skills, knowledge and a strategy with an edge or some competitive advantage. You need to have a mindset that is resilient, that allows you to take risk, navigate uncertainty, manage the pressures and stresses of the trading environment and its results orientation. You need to have the levels of awareness required to manage your thoughts and emotions and to be able to regulate your own trading behaviour, to be able to sustain focus, resist the temptations to react on impulses and reduce the impact of behavioural tendencies and biological responses. A strong psychological approach is integral to producing consistent and successful trading performance, to maximise the returns on your trading strategy.

The Rise of Trading Psychology

When I began working in sports psychology in the early 2000s it was in its relevant infancy in the UK, although in eastern Europe, the USA and Australia it was far more developed. The mindset of many sports people was that sports psychology was for people who had performance dysfunction, or clinical issues – it was seen as pathological. Very few sports people talked about visiting the sports psychologist and many teams did not at that time fully utilise or embrace sports psychology. Over the years that mindset has shifted significantly to the point where sports psychologists are available to most athletes and teams; they are used openly and recognised as part of the coaching and performance team. This behavioural shift has largely been down to the evolution of the drive by teams and athletes to seek every possible advantage when they are competing, the rise in the popularity of psychology in general and the move of the sports psychologist's role from being about fixing problems (pathological) to enhancing performance. This pattern is similar in trading, where even since my first involvement in early 2005 I have seen the attitudes of traders towards psychology move from strong scepticism to being much more open and embracing. The global market events of 2008 and the challenges of trading the markets in the years since that time may have helped somewhat in this evolution, alongside the rise in popularity of behavioural finance and the increasing number of academic studies and books that focus on financial decision making and its psychological aspects.

With this rise in interest in trading psychology, more and more traders have realised, or perhaps admitted, that being able to develop their psychological approach would have benefits on their trading decisions, performance and profits. More traders are open to reading about trading psychology, attending workshops or having one-to-one coaching than ever, even though some may still be hesitant or sceptical. This growing trend was identified in an online article published by Reuters in September 2012 entitled "FX traders seek coaching in battle for dominance"[2] and in an article entitled "Finding your inner trader"[3] published in *Bloomberg Markets Magazine* (April 2014):

In the take-no-prisoners world of foreign exchange dealing, asking traders to look inside themselves and confront their inner demons may seem a forlorn endeavour. Yet some banks are turning to performance coaches to give their traders an edge in the battle to make money in the $4.5 trillion dollar a day FX market. This soft skills approach contrasts with the popular stereotype of FX traders hurling prices – and abuse – at each other across the dealing room floor. But while some dismiss techniques to develop a 'clear-headed space' in which to trade as touchy-feely gimmickry, many are keen to embrace any tactic to outwit other market participants, whether human or machine.

"FX traders seek coaching in battle
for dominance", Reuters

If you are reading this then it is pretty likely that you are, at a minimum, slightly curious about how you could improve your trading performance via the use of psychological approaches, or you may be further along the continuum – a convert to trading psychology but looking for a different approach or methodology to help you overcome the challenges you face. Whichever you are, *TraderMind* provides an opportunity for you to develop your mental and emotional skills and to enhance your trading psychology skills, and enhance your decision-making process and market returns.

The New Contenders: Neuroscience and Mindfulness

Over the years, trading psychology has evolved. In its early stages, understanding and approaches were derived primarily from existing cognitive, behavioural and performance-based psychological approaches. Then we saw the introduction and rapid uptake of interest in behavioural finance, behavioural economics and decision science. More recently, growing interest in the human brain has seen the rise of neuroscience and its trading and investing derivatives, neurofinance and neuroeconomics. Over the years, in my own practice as a coach I have adapted and refined my approaches based on new thinking, research and my own experiences in "real-time" work with traders. Since 2010 I have become more and more interested in the trading brain and how neuroscience can be applied to enhance trading and investing performance. Whilst reading and researching in articles, books and journals I kept coming across one word, *mindfulness*. There is a large volume of neuroscience research that is based on looking at mindfulness and its impact on the brain, and mindfulness was often offered as a practical application or intervention at the end of articles or papers looking at the regulation of emotion or attention, for example. Over time, the frequency of my exposure to mindfulness increased and my interest developed, and then, following a coincidental presentation I attended on mindfulness for coaches at a conference, I started my own practice and training, leading over the years to my training as a mindfulness teacher.

Mindfulness is a way of paying attention, in the present moment, to yourself, others and the world around you. It is a skill that can be learnt and, as you will discover in this book, the research shows that people who practise mindfulness benefit in many ways including improved attention and concentration, enhanced emotional regulation, a greater awareness of their thoughts and emotions, lower levels of impulsivity, lower sensitivity to biases and habitual behaviours, enhanced risk-based decision making and – from a health perspective – improved immune system functioning. Mindfulness can not only be practised through formal meditation-type practices but also by incorporating its key principles and approaches, and shorter practices, into everyday life, both in and out of the markets.

TraderMind provides an evolved, very practical and applied approach to trading psychology, focused upon the use of mindfulness-based approaches.

TraderMind

TraderMind has been written as a result of the evolution of my own approaches to working with traders and fund managers, both in individual and group sessions, which, over recent years, has seen me incorporate mindfulness-based approaches into my repertoire in an attempt to increase my effectiveness with clients and the results that they achieve. As you will discover later in the book, the use of mindfulness-based approaches is growing in many performance-orientated areas including sports, the military, law enforcement, trauma medicine and in corporate leadership programmes. The use of such approaches is slowly growing in trading, with early adopters including Ray Dalio, founder of $130 billion hedge fund firm Bridgewater Associates: "Meditation more than anything in my life was the biggest ingredient for whatever success I've had", he said in an interview at Georgetown University in the USA in October 2011. As reported in Reuters: "Meditation gives me a centeredness, it gives me an ability to look at things without the emotional hijacking, without the ego, in a way that gives me a certain clarity."[4] Dalio says that the practice has been useful for him, both for generating creative thought and evaluating and responding to the huge overload of stimulus which presses upon a money manager every day. Bill Gross, the bond giant of Pimco, says that he leaves the trading floor every day for yoga and meditation. Importantly, meditation is being seen more and more as an edge for traders, a theme that was reported in "How to make a killing on Wall Street, start meditating",[5] which gave examples of billionaire hedge fund trader Paul Tudor-Jones as a convert to meditation, the introduction of mindfulness programmes at Goldman Sachs and a key quote from Jeff Walker, former head of JPMorgan Chase & Co.'s private equity unit and a long-time meditator who stated about traders: "These guys are saying, 'There's an edge here that I need.'"

It is important to stress here that mindfulness-based approaches can incorporate meditation-type practices but also offer more informal and non-typical meditation-based methods that can be utilised as well, and importantly that the word *meditation* could be substituted with equal meaning for "mind training" or even "mind fitness training" as used in military and law-enforcement settings, and often in my own work with traders and investors.

TraderMind makes the case for the use of mindfulness-based approaches to enhance trader performance, based upon research and practical applications in the real world of the markets. It seeks to teach you specific approaches, practices and techniques that will help you to build the skills of awareness and attention, which will enable you to manage your thoughts and emotions more effectively, overcome habitual or impulsive trading behaviours that are not useful, manage your feelings of energy, develop your market feel and intuition, become more responsive to the market, become more situationally aware and build patterns of effective trading behaviour, as well as overcoming behavioural biases and ultimately enhancing your trading decisions.

The approaches that you will learn from *TraderMind* can be utilised on their own as a core approach to trading psychology or they can sit alongside other approaches and methods as a complementary strategy.

Having a strong trading psychology does not, of course, replace the need for trading skills, knowledge, strategy or key performance behaviours such as preparation and performance analysis, but rather acts as an enabler or facilitator, even a multiplier, of enhanced trader decision making and improved performance. The best traders and investors have a combination of skills and knowledge, strategy and psychology.

What's in Store?

Chapter 1: What is Mindfulness?

In this chapter we explore what mindfulness is and what it isn't. We look at the rise of mindfulness from its Buddhist origins to its use in elite sport, leadership, the military and the markets. We also look at the research into the benefits that mindfulness practice provides, including how it can help with managing emotions, improving attention, reducing stress reactivity, enhancing decision making and boosting health.

Chapter 2: Developing Your Mindfulness Muscle

When I teach mindfulness I often talk about it as "mind fitness", having a mind that is fit for action and capable of performing well in the trading environment. Developing mental and emotional fitness is much like developing physical fitness, requiring time and practice. In this chapter we look at the concept of neuroplasticity – how the brain can grow and develop through training – and learn specific methods for developing the skill of mindfulness. You will also get to take the *Mindful Attention and Awareness Scale*, so that you can assess your current level of mindfulness.

Chapter 3: The Attention and Awareness Advantage

Without well-developed attention it is very difficult to do anything well, be it reading, having a conversation, playing an instrument, playing sport or trading the markets. Attention lies at the heart of trading performance, and is also at the heart of mindfulness practice. In this chapter you will learn about the three key areas of attention and how to develop your attention and awareness through mindfulness practice, leading to a greater ability to sustain attention, recover more quickly from distraction, be more situationally aware, develop greater empathy and also develop greater self-control and self-regulation; the ability to manage your thoughts and emotions.

Chapter 4: Thinking About Thinking

Your thoughts, beliefs and perceptions all influence your trading and investing behaviour and subsequent decision making. Having a greater awareness of your thinking processes, and being able to manage your thoughts more effectively, can lead to improved decision making. In this chapter we look at strategies for developing thought awareness and techniques for working with thoughts, beliefs and perceptions that may be interfering with your trading performance.

Chapter 5: Embracing Emotions

Emotions get a lot of coverage in writing and conversations about trading. Over the last few years we have seen some significant shifts in how emotions are viewed in trading, and in the ways in which emotions can be most effectively managed. Being more open to your emotions, embracing them and working with them, in line with the latest neuroscience research is the key theme and focus of the practices in this chapter.

Chapter 6: Managing Urges and Impulses

Warren Buffett talks about the need for traders and investors to be able to overcome the urges that get people into trouble in the markets, and that is the theme of this chapter. What are the urges and impulses that traders face, where do they come from and how can they be managed more effectively?

Chapter 7: Trading With the Body in Mind

The brain and body are not two separate entities as many people have come to believe; rather, the brain is "embodied" within the body and they are a part of one integrated system. In this chapter we look at the "physical" side of trading, the sensing and feeling of the markets physiologically, the evolutionary benefits of this and how to apply them to the markets. We also look at the importance of physical and cognitive energy and their impact on your decision process.

Chapter 8: Habits, Behaviour, Action

At the heart of all trading decisions lies trading behaviour – action. Many of these actions are "habits", well-established patterns of behaviour, some of which serve you well and others of which may be creating interference in your performance. In this chapter we explore how behaviours and habits are established, how to build ones that are effective for trading and how to manage and release existing habits that are no longer useful.

Chapter 9: Turning Towards Difficulty

Trading brings many challenges, not least having to deal with losses, losing runs, change and other causes of trading stress. All traders will face periods of difficulty in their career, some more intense than others, some for longer than others. In this chapter we explore the use of mindfulness-based approaches for dealing with difficulties, including the importance (and benefit) of turning towards them and approaching them, rather than avoiding them.

Chapter 10: The Mindful Trader and Investor

This chapter focuses on helping you to develop your own ongoing mindfulness practice, both formal and informal, and explores ways to apply it in real time, during the trading day, helping you to become a mindful trader.

TraderMind Mindfulness-Based Trading and Investing Training Programme

The book concludes with a template for an 8-week *TraderMind* training programme, with a specific focus for each week and recommended exercises and reading to complete. Taking the time to complete the programme will provide you with a formalised training programme and enable you to integrate all the knowledge and strategies from the book, develop your skills and maximise the benefits you get from your purchase. (The programme is supplemented by access to several online resources that will complement your training experience and learning.)

Getting the Most From *TraderMind*

One of the key factors in the success of any coaching, training or development programme is how much effort the client puts into it, and likewise one of the factors that will determine how successful *TraderMind* is in helping you to enhance your trading performance will be how fully you immerse yourself in the book and the action you take as a result of it. As my father has always told me, "you get out what you put in".

Here are a few key points to help you get the most out of *TraderMind*:

- Remain curious and open minded; there are some relatively new approaches in this book that may be unfamiliar to you at first – they were to me once. Keep an open mind and try ideas out first before making any judgements.
- *TraderMind* is a skills-based programme; to get the most from it will require effort and commitment. Just like developing any skill, practice and time are required.
- Utility – everyone who reads this book will be different in some way. As you go through the book take out what is useful (workable) for you in relation to what you are trying to achieve in your trading. Think in terms of utility, what is useful or not, rather than right or wrong.
- Keep your expectations reasonable and manageable to increase your chance of success.
- Remember that enhancing performance is evolutionary and not revolutionary – work at learning the key content and ideas from the book, practise the exercises and techniques, and keep looking for signs of progress.

What Brings You To This Book?

Take a moment to sit quietly in a comfortable position. Ask yourself "*What brings me to this book?*" Notice what answers come to mind.

Sit quietly for a bit longer and when you are ready, ask yourself the question again. "*What brings me to this book?*" Allow yourself to be aware of your thoughts and answers.

And when you are ready, ask yourself for the final time. "*What brings me to this book?*"

Final Words

I know that the many traders and fund managers I have worked with across the globe, both in group training programmes and in one-to-one coaching, have found the mindfulness-based approach to trading psychology refreshing, simple to apply and, most importantly, very effective. The feedback after workshops and training programmes that I run always cites the mindfulness techniques as being "very practical", "very useful" and amongst the key take-outs for action. It is because of this feedback, and the highly positive experiences of traders to whom I have taught mindfulness-based approaches in one-to-one coaching, that I have committed the time and effort to write this book. My aim is to make this type of approach available to a wider audience, whilst also providing further reading for course delegates and coaching clients who always ask "Is there a book I could read that you would recommend?"

Let me know how it goes.

1

What is Mindfulness?

What is Mindfulness?

Mindfulness is defined by one of the world's leading mindfulness researchers and practitioners, Jon Kabat-Zinn of the University of Massachusetts Medical School, as *"A way of paying attention: on purpose, in the present moment and non-judgementally to whatever arises in the field of your experience"*.[1] Michael Chaskalson, in his book *The Mindful Workplace*,[2] defines it as *"A way of paying attention in the present moment, to yourself, others and the world around you"*. In a very simple way, it is noticing what's happening, while it's happening. Mindfulness is a way of connecting to your present moment experience in an accepting way.

In trading, these definitions might translate behaviourally as trading in the moment, paying attention to what the market is doing right now and the environment around you, being aware of your own thoughts, emotions, physical sensations and any impulses or tendencies to act. You would be fully present and more aware of preconceived ideas or biases that could influence you, and you would probably be experiencing lower levels of anxiety as a result. You would be attentive and aware, responsive and engaged.

Mindfulness is the opposite of mindlessness, which can be defined as living on autopilot, governed by your past conditioning of thoughts, beliefs, emotional responses and behaviour. Whilst much of the time this process can be healthy and performance enhancing, within all of your automatic experiences there may also lie patterns of thinking, feeling and doing that are detrimental to your trading performance, ones that have been learnt in the past but are no longer useful.

The cultivation of mindfulness develops your ability to be present, to be aware of what is going on within you and around you, to notice the stream of moment-to-moment change and to develop greater choice, to act on purpose as opposed to being reactionary and dominated by mindless habits, patterns and reactivity.

Importantly, mindfulness is a skill – it can be learnt and developed. We all have an inherent ability to be mindful; however, with the ever-increasing pace of change in the world, the amount of instant stimulation and the level of information overload that our brains get exposed to, sometimes being mindful – whilst so simple in nature – can be extraordinarily difficult. Consider the requirements of the trading environment and its demands on your attention at any given time: prices flickering, P&L numbers moving, graphs and charts changing, news flowing from screens, squawks and televisions, the noise from other traders around you, phones, mobile phones, instant messenger... the list could go on, and the effect is that being able to be fully present, attending to the here and now, is, for many people, becoming more and more difficult.

The practice of mindfulness encompasses focusing your attention on your experience of thoughts, emotions, feelings and body sensations as they arise and pass, from moment to moment.

The Contact Points practice below is a great way to experience mindfulness.

Practice: Contact Points

- Find a comfortable, upright sitting position with your feet flat on the floor and your back slightly away from the back of the chair.
- You may choose to close your eyes or you may wish to keep them open, in which case, lower your gaze towards the floor.
- Focus your attention on to a physical sensation, the sensation of your body pressing down in contact with your chair, or the sensations in your feet as they contact the floor. Notice where the sensations are strongest, the feeling of sitting on the chair, or the contact of feet on the floor, and allow your attention to rest there.
- After a while you may find that your mind wanders. When you notice this, simply acknowledge where it has wandered to and bring your attention back to the contact point without judging or being critical. Minds wander, it is what they do.
- After a minute or two, let your eyes open and return your focus back to the room.

What was your experience like? Many people find that even in just a short time their mind wanders a number of times, to a number of different places, and often quite shortly after they begin.

This is probably a good point at which to switch our focus onto what mindfulness isn't. Despite all the potential benefits and upside to developing mindfulness skills to enhance your trading performance, there are still some people who remain a little wary of the idea, particularly when they think of it alongside the word "meditation". Here are some key points drawn from Mark Williams and Danny Penman's book *Mindfulness: A Practical Guide to Finding Peace in a Frantic World*:[3]

- Mindfulness is secular, and is not a religion. It is simply a form of mental training. To help frame it as such, the US Marines have named their mindfulness-based programme "Mind Fitness", as has a colleague of mine who delivers his programme in prisons, and as have I in my work with traders.

- Mindfulness practice is not a "soft" approach to mental training and will not deaden your mind or prevent you from striving towards achieving your trading goals. It will actually do the opposite, by training your mind, making it sharper and more effective and giving you a greater chance of achieving your goals.
- Mindfulness practice can be done seated, on buses or the train, while walking, and does not require any specific kind of clothing. You do not need to sit cross-legged in loose clothing or a kaftan, as seen in many magazines.
- Mindfulness is not complicated. It is a process, and there is no measure of success or failure in your practice of it. Even when your mindfulness practice feels difficult, you will find that you have gained something from it.
- Mindfulness practice does not have to take a lot of time, as you will see in Chapter 2. However, like learning any skill it does require some practice and perseverance if you are going to get the benefit.

Equanimity: Approaching and Acceptance vs. Avoidance and Aversion

One of the central and most important aspects of mindfulness-based approaches is accepting and approaching thoughts, emotions, impulses and behaviours rather than seeking to avoid them, or control them. This can, at first, seem a very counterintuitive approach, and for many an uncomfortable one, especially when you look at it in relation to more traditional psychological methodologies. However, as we shall see in later chapters, there is strong evidence that the suppression of thoughts and feelings is not a workable strategy and that being more open to them, accepting them and relating to them differently is far more effective.

Acceptance-based psychological approaches have been applied to performance populations including athletes and sports teams, and also to international chess players. In a study involving high-ranked chess players,[4] participants showed significant reductions in the interference of general, "unpleasant" thoughts, feelings, emotions and impulses during competitions as well as reductions in the frequency of their counterproductive reactions to these experiences as a result of learning strategies and techniques to accept and approach rather than avoid them. Also, as indicated by an objective chess performance measure, all participants in the experiment improved their performance during the 7 months after the protocol in comparison with the 7 months prior to it. In contrast, none of the control participants improved their chess performance.

Another study with a US college volleyball team found that after training in acceptance-based psychological skills, although their levels of performance anxiety remained similar pre- and post-study, they actually improved their performance quite significantly.[5] It was not so much the feeling of anxiety that was interfering with their performance, but how they were reacting to that feeling.

This process of accepting something, such as your thoughts or feelings, without resistance is referred to as "equanimity". In fact, in its wider sense, it refers to accepting things that you cannot control, to change what you can, but to let go of the struggle to change what you can't. You cannot, for example, control the markets. It is important to stress here that acceptance is not a passive state of resignation, and does not mean that you stop trying to grow and develop as a trader. Rather, acceptance entails a willingness to see things as they actually are in the present – in that moment – to experience them as they are. In my own work I often use the word "approaching" when talking about acceptance, to highlight that it is not a passive process, and that it is also about moving towards what we are experiencing rather than away from it. This ability to *approach* experience, especially when it is viewed as *unpleasant*, is particularly important in dealing with the thoughts, emotions and sensations in the moment, but also in encouraging exposure to these *difficult events* and ultimately it produces an increase in resilience and toughness.

Take a moment to reflect on what you have done up to now in an attempt to overcome the challenges faced in your own trading.

What Have You Done So Far To Improve Your Trading Psychology?

What have you already tried to get rid of your negative thoughts, emotions and ill-disciplined trading behaviours?

What have you already tried to reduce the impact of behavioural biases on your trading decisions?

Did you succeed in permanently getting rid of them?

What has this cost you? Time, effort, money?

Has this brought you closer to where you want to be with your trading?

The notion of approaching, moving towards thoughts, emotions and experiences rather than seeking to control or avoid them can be likened to falling into quicksand. If you were to fall into quicksand what would your instinctive reaction be? To struggle and try to fight your way out. And what would happen then? You would start to sink faster. So what is the correct process for surviving quicksand? Try to lay yourself out flat on your back, and stay as still and as calm as possible. Completely counter-intuitive, just like letting go of the struggle to control or avoid emotions, thoughts and experiences. The current movement towards being open to our internal experience is echoed in the following quote from Gardner and Moore in their book *The Psychology of Enhancing Human Performance*:[6]

Over the past several years an increasing body of literature has questioned the position that internal attempts to suppress or control unwanted thoughts or emotions have a paradoxical effect and may also lead to more frequent unwanted thoughts and emotions.

Acceptance keeps your focus on the task; there is no need to escape or control or avoid your internal experience. The struggle to be without distress is the problem, not the presence of these thoughts and emotions.

Impermanence

No man ever steps in the same river twice, for it's not the same river and he's not the same man.

Heraclitus

We like certainty. We like stability. We like to think that we can control things. But, because everything is always changing, that approach doesn't really work. In mindfulness a key principle is that of impermanence, that everything is in a constant state of change, and that nothing lasts forever. Your thoughts, emotions and physical sensations are constantly shifting and changing, a bit like the weather coming and going, and the markets are dynamic and shifting and changing from day to day.

One of the biggest challenges for traders is learning to cope with the uncertainty of the markets, when most humans naturally favour certainty. Uncertainty often brings a feeling of anxiety with it, and by being able to see the markets as impermanent, in accepting the uncertainty of their nature, you can bring a different perception – mindset – with you to the markets that will reduce these feelings of anxiety, and help you to navigate the fluctuating conditions more effectively.

Understanding this principle of impermanence is also very helpful in realising that, as Mark Douglas puts it in his book *Trading in the Zone,*[7] *"every moment in the market is unique"*. This principle has implications for our traditional sense of trading discipline, best summed up by the phrase *"have a plan, and trade the plan"*. Because the market is dynamic and shifting, preconceived plans may lose some validity and effectiveness once you have entered the market and are holding a position. Rigidly sticking to your trading plan once the conditions have changed would be like soldiers sticking to a mission plan despite receiving intelligence that the battle environment had changed, or a sports team sticking to a game plan that is not working. Holding on to the idea of impermanence can help you to be more flexible, to reduce the need to hang onto positions and plans despite the most effective action being to change them. This mindset is key to developing your judgement, your ability to make – in the moment – trading and investing decisions that reflect the current market environment.

Over the longer term the principle of impermanence becomes important because it is helpful to recognise that any winning or losing runs are impermanent, that any changes in the market are impermanent, that any changes to your performance are impermanent. Nothing stays the same forever. Life and the markets are uncertain, and by embracing that you can change your experience of them for the better.

Mindfulness in the Markets

Applying mindfulness in real time in the markets involves three key dimensions (Figure 1.1): a focus of attention on and awareness of the moment; an acceptance of and approach to your experience in that moment; and a focus on taking effective action for the situation you are in. These processes can be applied discretely in real time by actively applying specific techniques or strategies, or can come in a more natural form as a result of shifts to how you think, feel and behave that are the result of your formal mindfulness practice and the changes in your brain, and hence your performance, that it brings.

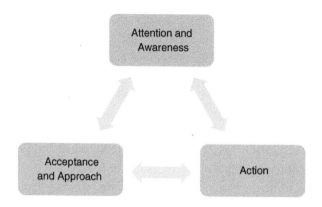

Figure 1.1 The three dimensions of applying mindfulness in the markets.

From Buddha to Boardroom to Battlefield – the Rise of Mindfulness

I first came across the term "mindfulness" when researching and reading on the topic of neuroscience and became increasingly aware of references to, and studies centred around, mindfulness. The more I read the more I became intrigued and curious, and eventually that curiosity took me to training in mindfulness for myself. When I began to learn and practise mindfulness for myself I was very pleasantly surprised that on the first course I attended, the very first exercise – a mindfulness of breath practice – was exactly the same as the attention training exercise that I used with athletes in my sports psychology consulting. It is interesting when you look at the evolution of mindfulness that it has moved quite quickly over recent years from its "spiritual" meditation-based Buddhist roots, through academic research, into medicine (the Mindfulness-Based Stress Reduction programme founded by Jon Kabat-Zinn at the University of Massachusetts Medical School is recognised as a mainstream clinical intervention for people suffering with anxiety, stress and depression), the sports and performance arena, leadership, law enforcement, medical trauma care and, as you will soon read about in the next part of this chapter, the military. Some companies have begun to offer "meditation" or "quiet" rooms where employees can go to meditate or reflect in quiet;

others have made meditation classes and even retreats available. Further along the spectrum are companies which have fully embraced the mindfulness movement and which provide not just rooms, meditation training and retreats, but also fully blown mindfulness-based programmes for their employees and leaders. Google brings mindfulness to its employees through its Search Inside Yourself (SIY) programme, which blends science, meditation and business, and this type of approach is being adopted more widely by other corporations. I believe it could also quite easily be adopted in the trading and investment community.

The popularity of mindfulness can be measured by the hugely increasing number of academic papers that have been published over recent years, and from my own experience in terms of the financial markets by the number of traders and portfolio managers I talk with who have taken up regular yoga or meditation practice. One trading group that I work with has embraced mindfulness practice, and now offers a daily 10-minute mindfulness session that is available for all traders to attend.

Michael Chaskalson puts the rise of mindfulness primarily down to two key factors. Firstly, secularisation – taking it from being almost exclusively a Buddhist meditative process; secondly, the growth in the science behind mindfulness and the subsequent volume of academic papers that have been published on the subject. The findings from these papers show a whole host of benefits for people who practise mindfulness

The Benefits of Mindfulness

In the 1980s the US Army conducted its Trojan Warrior Project,[8] where 25 Special Forces soldiers nicknamed *"Jedi Knights"* were given 6 months of extensive martial arts and meditation training that enabled them, as an outcome, to outperform their peers on psychological and biological feedback tests. Skip forward to 2008 and a group of 31 US Marine reservists training at the Marine Corps base in Quantico, Virginia, USA for deployment participated in an 8-week mindfulness course, meditating for an average of 12 minutes per day, being taught awareness and attention skills and yoga-based poses. Move forward again to 2011 and a report in the *Washington Times* is headlined "Marines expanding use of meditation training".[9] In that report they interviewed a Marine Staff Sergeant who had recently undergone pre-deployment training which featured weapons training, physical workouts, high-stress counter-insurgency simulations and weekly meditation classes. His feedback on the classes included the following comments:

A lot of people thought they would be a waste of time. Why are we sitting around a classroom doing this weird meditative stuff?

But over time, I felt more relaxed, I slept better. Physically, I noticed that I wasn't tense all the time. It helps you think more clearly and decisively in stressful situations. That was a benefit.

The mindfulness work done with the US Marines was led by former US Army Captain and current Georgetown Professor Elizabeth Stanley and Amishi Jha of the Department of Psychology Center for Cognitive Neuroscience at the University of Pennsylvania. The programme, which they called Mindfulness-Based Mind Fitness, aimed to improve soldier effectiveness by developing resilience and improving emotional health, mental performance and self-regulation in combat situations. The results of their study from 2008[10] demonstrated that compared with a control group of 17 Marines who had not participated in the study, the group had slept better and scored higher on emotional and cognitive evaluations. In real terms the impact included greater situational awareness, not having emotions driving behaviour and developing greater resilience to the stresses of combat.

The use of these approaches by the military is of particular interest to traders because of some of the core challenges in trading roles, namely making decisions under uncertainty, with the presence of risk, stress and pressure. Errors in decision making are a major cause of casualty in combat situations and so the pursuit of methodologies that can enhance this is a key focus for the military. The impact of using mindfulness-based approaches on improving this ability was highlighted by the research conducted with the US Marines by Jha and Stanley, who found that:

Mindfulness training safeguards them against distraction and emotional reactivity and lets them maintain a mental workspace that ensures quick and considered decisions and action.

Besides offering some protection to combatants from post-traumatic stress and other anxiety disorders, the mindfulness training enhanced the clarity of thinking needed for soldiers fighting in challenging and ambiguous counter-insurgency zones.

To be able to keep a high function of working memory (your real-time mental workspace and also a key component of your self-regulatory ability), be less emotionally reactive and think quickly and clearly amidst the uncertain and dynamic nature of the market is obviously highly desirable, as is being able to cope with the highs and lows of winning and losing and withstand the pressures of performance demands in institutions; all these require a strong psychological make-up. It is possible, through effective *mind fitness* or mental and emotional training, such as the exercises and approaches found in this book, to develop such a mindset.

A study published in 2011 entitled "Mindfulness practice leads to increases in regional brain gray matter density",[11] which investigated pre- and post-training changes in brain grey matter concentration following participation in an 8-week Mindfulness-Based Stress Reduction (MBSR) programme, stated some dramatic and beneficial changes. It showed that after the 8 weeks of mindfulness training there were significant increases in gray matter concentration in the regions of the brain that are involved with learning and memory processes, emotional regulation, self-referential processing and perspective taking.

The MBSR programme originated at the Stress Reduction Clinic at the University of Massachusetts Medical School in 1979 through founder Dr Jon Kabat-Zinn and his team. The MBSR programme is now a fully recognised worldwide clinical programme for managing stress, anxiety and depression in particular, and has been, along with various evolutionary variations, researched extensively. In 2010 the Mental Health Foundation published its *Mindfulness Report*,[12] a review of the current studies and papers on mindfulness which highlighted many of the key benefits attributable to mindfulness practice, including:

- Being less likely to experience psychological distress, having lower levels of stress and being less neurotic.
- Having a greater awareness, understanding and acceptance of emotions and a quicker recovery from bad moods.
- Having less frequent negative thoughts and being more able to let go of them when they arise.
- Having higher and more stable self-esteem and being less dependent on external factors.
- Being less likely to react defensively or aggressively when feeling threatened.
- Having good social skills.
- Having increased self-awareness.
- Having higher success in achieving academic and personal goals.
- Having improved attention, job performance, productivity and satisfaction.
- Feeling more in control of behaviour and more able to manage internal thoughts and feelings and resist acting on impulse.
- Having reduced addictive behaviours – drugs, alcohol or caffeine.

There were social and relationship benefits in the form of better communication, stronger relationships and less relationship conflict. From a health perspective the report showed benefits in terms of increased blood flow, reduced blood pressure, a reduced risk of cardiovascular disease, fewer hospital admissions, fewer visits to the doctor and greater reported health and well-being from people who were higher in mindfulness.

As can be seen from the results of these studies alone, the benefits of practising mindfulness and developing mind fitness are numerous, and of potentially very significant benefit for traders and fund managers. Ellen Langer, who has been researching mindfulness for nearly 40 years, has found that for almost any measure, mindfulness generates a more positive result and she says that at the very highest level in any field – CEOs, artists, musicians, athletes, teachers, mechanics – you will find mindful people.[13]

One of the key findings by Jha and Stanley in their studies with the US Marines was the positive impact of mind fitness training on working memory, which can be thought of as the short-term scratch pad system you use to manage relevant information, solve real-time problems and importantly regulate emotions and behaviour. Working memory suffers from depletion under heavy cognitive load and stress, but with regular mind fitness training, soldiers' thinking and decision making was enhanced. The maintenance of working memory under market stress is key for traders and enables them to stay focused on effective action, whilst being situationally aware, mentally flexible and, where appropriate, responding flexibly.

Another key outcome, and again key to decision-making capability, was the soldiers' ability to regulate their emotions, particularly in situations where the fight-or-flight stress response is activated. This activation leads to evolutionary processes occurring – such as pupils dilating, heart rate and breathing increasing, blood flowing from the stomach and into the muscles (the feeling of butterflies) and stress hormones such as cortisol flowing through the body. Making good decisions can be difficult in these situations as blood flow is redirected from the prefrontal cortex, where thinking, decision making and analysis occur to the limbic system and brain stem, which is more associated with instinct and survival. Soldiers who underwent mind fitness training were less reactive to threat situations, den.. strating an ability to think more clearly, act more effectively and be more responsive to their situational demands. As we will discover later in the book, higher levels of mindfulness have been linked to higher levels of resilience.

The research from the use of mind fitness approaches with the US military, although not extensive or conclusive, and subject to future research and expansion of the programme, does, however, demonstrate some verifiable positive outcomes and opportunities for performance enhancement for traders who have some similarity of decision-making challenges. How, then, does this relate specifically to traders and the demands of trading the financial markets?

Becoming more mindful has many potential benefits for traders, as we have seen, but there are also other key and important benefits that mindfulness research with traders is demonstrating, specifically in helping traders to be less impacted by some of the behavioural finance biases – such as the disposition effect (selling winners too early and running losses too far) and loss aversion.

In a presentation at the NeuroPsychoEconomics Conference 2012, Mark van Overveld of Rotterdam School of Management shared some key findings of his research using simple mindfulness-based interventions to enhance trader decision making.[14] Among his key findings were:

- Mindfulness is associated with changes in areas of the brain relating to emotion regulation, response control and deliberate decision making.
- Mindfulness seems very relevant for traders.
- Mindfulness increased attention.
- Feelings of stress were reduced.
- Managing emotions (such as fear and anger) was improved.
- Traders learnt to accept emotions instead of acting on them.
- Awareness of emotions allows for adequate emotion regulation.

- Mindfulness facilitated financial decision making in terms of risk taking and timely loss aversion.
- Mindfulness helped individuals balance risk taking and loss prevention.

An interesting study from researchers at INSEAD and The Wharton School[15] found that just one 15-minute focused-breathing meditation can help people to improve their decision making, including cutting losses in stocks. One of the challenges to cutting losses is that people have trouble admitting that they are wrong and don't want to feel that their time and effort in planning the trade or investment was a waste of time; so they often take additional risk to see if they can at least get back to break even. The study found that performing a brief mindfulness practice before making the decision encouraged people to take in more information from the present moment and reduced the amount of focus people placed on the past and the future, which led to less *negative* emotion which then enabled them to be able to *let go* of their trades more easily. The mindfulness practice had produced a debiasing effect.

One of the core elements of mindfulness is holding a non-judgemental awareness. This does not mean in any way that if you are mindful you do not make judgements *per se*, but rather that the manner in which they are made is less critical than perhaps many people may experience. This ability to hold a present-moment, non-judgemental mindset is demonstrated by George Soros, who indicates that one of his key strengths is his ability to non-judgementally reflect on his investment decisions. Being able to cultivate opinions and views is very important for traders and investors, but being able to do so without strong attachment, high ego and with a sense of impermanence and flexibility is even more so. Mindfulness practice can help to develop this mindset.

Another challenge facing traders and fund managers is information overload and high distractibility. There is an unprecedented amount of information and distraction in the trading environment – screens, charts, instant messenger, phones, televisions, squawk boxes, newspapers, websites, emails, texts and other traders. To some degree information is useful, but for all of us there is a point at which we start to get overloaded, which results in activation of the stress response, leading to a reduction in brain function as your *survival brain* takes over from your *thinking brain*. It then becomes difficult to make decisions, to plan, to be flexible, ... even to remember. Mindfulness helps to reduce stress reactivity, to reduce the impact of information overload, and may help with being able to see with greater clarity what information is important to focus on and what is not. With research from the Centre for Creative Leadership[16] showing that the average worker is interrupted every 11 minutes and that it may take up to 25 minutes for that person to fully refocus again, the ability to sustain attention, recognise when you are distracted and refocus quickly – which are key outcomes of mindfulness training – have significant importance.

Mindfulness is new for the majority of traders and fund managers I work with, although a small but growing proportion of them have participated in yoga, and some more formalised meditation practices as we saw in the Introduction with both leading hedge fund traders Ray Dalio of Bridgewater Capital and Bill Gross of Pimco. At a recent conference in Japan where I was talking to traders and fund managers on enhancing decision making, and at which I presented a section on the benefits of mindfulness training, I was introduced to members of a very successful fund based in New York which places high emphasis on its team's use of yoga and mindfulness-based practice. They felt that this provided them with the calm and focused mindsets required to make their investment decisions and also had a very positive impact on their own personal health and well-being. A very holistic philosophy towards investing performance.

Mindfulness training can then potentially help traders to make better decisions under conditions of uncertainty, to cope with the pressures of performance and risk taking, to deal with winning and losing more effectively and to manage the general stresses associated with the trading environment.

TraderMind: Mindfulness-Based Trading and Investing

Building mind-fitness with mindfulness training may help anyone who must maintain peak performance in the face of extremely stressful circumstances, from first responders, relief workers and trauma surgeons to professional and Olympic athletes.

Associate Professor Amishi Jha, University of Miami[17]

TraderMind provides a psychological framework for traders and investors that is centred around the practice of mindfulness-based approaches. Whilst I use mindfulness as part of a wider toolkit and approach, I really believe that many people would benefit from applying mindfulness in their own trading and investing based on the following four points:

1 Mindfulness has been the subject of extensive neuroscience research and although it is often noted that the quality of this research does vary, there have been many excellent studies.
2 There is a growing use of this type of methodology among performance areas such as the military, law enforcement, elite sport and leadership programmes.
3 These are practical strategies that can be practised and developed just like any other skill.
4 They provide a wide range of benefits from a core set of practices and so offer a real bang-for-buck investment for time-pressed traders and fund managers.

TraderMind is focused on teaching traders and fund managers specific approaches, practices and techniques that will help them to meet more effectively the challenges of trading and investing. To be able to meet these challenges, a specific set of psychological characteristics is required, as identified in Figure 1.2 and explained below – the five components of *TraderMind*.

1 *Attention and Awareness*

Attention and awareness are core to trading and investing performance and develop your ability to focus and concentrate

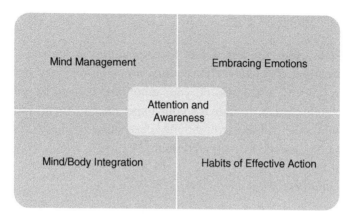

Figure 1.2 The five components of *TraderMind*.

on relevant market cues and information, to be able to sustain that concentration over extended periods of time, to recognise when you have become distracted – perhaps by market noise or inner noise – and then be able to refocus. Attention and awareness are also key because they are fundamental skills to develop in order to self-regulate, to be able to manage your thoughts, emotions and behaviour; they also contribute significantly to your powers of self-control. Awareness has two dimensions: firstly, noticing what you are thinking, feeling and doing, an internal awareness; secondly, an external, situational awareness, the ability to be aware of what is going on around you, to be able to assess and absorb information from the external environment effectively and respond to it appropriately. Situational awareness is largely taught and discussed amongst military circles but is, for me, a fundamental trading skill.

2   *Mind Management*

Mind management is your ability to work with and manage your thinking processes. To have an awareness of your thoughts, beliefs and perceptions and to be able to work with them and relate to them in such a way that any potential detrimental impact is reduced.

3   *Embracing Emotions*

Embracing emotions refers to your ability to manage your emotions effectively. This requires you to be able to recognise, to have an awareness of, your emotions; then to be able to regulate them, to manage your experience of them. Fundamental to embracing emotions is accepting them, approaching them and working with them.

4   *Mind/Body Integration*

Contrary to an evolving popular belief, the mind and body are an integrated system, with one affecting the other. In *Trader-Mind*, traders are encouraged and shown how to improve the connectivity between the two systems to improve decision making by enhancing your awareness of your bodily sensations and responses to feelings that can be indicators of risk and reward in the markets. The connection between a healthy body and a healthy mind is also important, with neuroscience research demonstrating the strong impact of energy levels and fatigue, for example, on your decision-making process.

5   *Habits of Effective Action*

At the core of any decision is action, it is the only way in which you can make or lose money in the markets. Action is also key because the daily habitual patterns of behaviour that we all have can either be contributing to or detracting from your market returns. Building habits of effective action – those that support your values, goals and trading mission – can help to reduce the impact of your thoughts and feelings on your trading, acting in a preventative way. Being able to recognise, and release, ineffective habits is also important in *TraderMind*.

A phrase that really captures the essence of what having high levels of mindfulness or mind fitness means for traders is the following: "*Mindfulness practice promotes mindful responding as opposed to mindless reacting to events.*" Responding to the markets and to any relevant sources of information, as the situation unfolds, rather than simply reacting to internal thoughts, emotions and feelings in the moment. *TraderMind* is focused on developing the five components above through a mindfulness-based approach.

Developing Mindfulness

Having worked with many traders and portfolio managers across the globe, teaching mindfulness-based approaches as part of my overall approach to trading performance and psychology, I can assure you that the allure of the potential benefits is, for most participants, enough to gain their curiosity and get them to engage, even if tentatively to begin with, in what for many are initially perceived as *weird* mental training practices. Interestingly, post-course and coaching feedback often indicates the mindfulness-based approaches and techniques as being key take-aways for attendees. The one downfall for some is that, like any skill, to develop it requires time and effort. However, research into the use of mindfulness-based approaches in trading does suggest that even short interventions and techniques can be very useful. You can also benefit greatly just from simply knowing some of the key mindfulness-based principles, by seeing things differently, and also by utilising some of the 'in-the-moment' strategies from within this book and bringing short mindful moments into your trading and investing day.

In the chapters that follow you will be shown how to develop the five key components of *TraderMind*. You will be introduced to the core skills and approaches, including mindful awareness and attention, how to work with your thoughts, managing emotions, building the mind/body connection, how to keep a focus on effective action and how to integrate the components into a psychological approach that can enhance your trading decisions and performance.

2

Developing Your Mindfulness Muscle

How Mindful are You?

Before we explore some of the techniques you can employ to develop your mindfulness ability, I would like to invite you to take the Mindful Attention Awareness Scale (MAAS) developed by Kirk Brown at Virginia Commonwealth University in Richmond, Virginia, USA, which will provide you with an indicator of your current level of mindfulness. Brown developed the MAAS as a graduate student to measure people's ability to notice their internal body signals – a process known as interoception – while recovering from medical challenges. A person who seemed more aware of their internal experience appeared to recover more quickly from medical procedures. MAAS scores correlate with physical and mental health and even the quality of relationships. In a study where health participants had to label the feeling of emotional facial expressions, higher dispositional mindfulness as measured by the MAAS predicted:

(a) Increased activation in the prefrontal cortex – the cognitive, *thinking* area of the brain.
(b) Reduced amygdala activity (the amygdala acts like radar within the brain and is very sensitive to threat and danger), resulting in lower stress reactivity.

(c) Stronger inhibitory association between amygdala activity and regions of the prefrontal cortex – which is important for emotional regulation.

People who score high on MAAS are more aware of their unconscious processes, have more cognitive control and a greater ability to shape what they do than people lower on the scale – they have greater mind fitness.

Please answer according to what really reflects your experience rather than what you think your experience should be.

1 = almost always
2 = very frequently
3 = somewhat frequently
4 = somewhat infrequently
5 = very infrequently
6 = almost never

1   I could be experiencing some emotion and not be conscious of it until some time later.
2   I break or spill things because of carelessness, not paying attention, or thinking of something else.
3   I find it difficult to stay focused on what's happening in the present.
4   I tend to walk quickly to get where I'm going without paying attention to what I experience along the way.
5   I tend not to notice feelings of physical tension or discomfort until they really grab my attention.
6   I forget a person's name almost as soon as I've been told it for the first time.
7   It seems I am "running on automatic" without much awareness of what I'm doing.
8   I rush through activities without being really attentive to them.
9   I get so focused on the goal I want to achieve that I lose touch with what I am doing right now to get there.
10   I do jobs or tasks automatically, without being aware of what I'm doing.
11   I find myself listening to someone with one ear, doing something else at the same time.

12 I drive places on "automatic pilot" and then wonder why I went there.
13 I find myself preoccupied with the future or the past.
14 I find myself doing things without paying attention.
15 I snack without being aware that I'm eating.

Source: Brown and Ryan (2003).[1]

When you have answered all 15 questions, add your scores together and then divide this total by 15 to get your average score per question. This is your MAAS score, where 1 is low and 6 is high.

I would encourage you to look at your scores both in terms of the overall score and the variance in your individual scores on each statement. Where did you tend to score low? Where did you tend to score high? Were there any surprises?

Once you know your MAAS score the obvious question is, how can I improve it? The answer to that is mindfulness training. After a period of 6 to 8 weeks of mindfulness-based training you can then retake the test and see what you notice in your responses to the statements.

Developing Your Mindfulness Muscle

If you wanted to get physically fitter how would you go about it? The course of action you take would be driven to some degree by your long-term goals, for example cardiovascular fitness, strength, flexibility, competitive fitness, but whichever end outcome you choose in order to get there would require you to undertake some level of physical training. How much exercise you did and how often you trained would be dependent on your goals. When you undertake physical training you stress your body's systems, and through a process known as overcompensation you grow fitter and stronger, your body adapts to the stress of exercise and you get a training effect. Ad hoc physical training would not produce any significant training effect; you need to exercise with some frequency, intensity and consistency to optimise your gains.

If you want to develop mindfulness, mind fitness, the process is essentially the same as for developing physical fitness, in that regular and consistent practice of the mind fitness training techniques and approaches is required (Figure 2.1). Mindfulness is a skill; it can be taught, learnt and developed. Physical training creates changes to your cardiovascular and musculoskeletal system. When you train your brain you create changes to the neural pathways that exist within the brain, and, as we saw in the study in Chapter 1, also to the actual density of the gray matter within your brain. This process of brain change is known as neuroplasticity. Dr Richard Davidson, a neuroscientist at the University of Wisconsin, Madison, Wisconsin, USA, has been researching mindfulness since the early 1990s and has demonstrated that mindfulness training changes the brain. As he says, *"The mental practice of meditation is having an effect on the brain in the same way that golf or tennis practice will enhance performance"*.[2] People high in mindfulness have levels of brain activation that are very different from the normal population – mindfulness training is the root to developing the mind fitness required to trade and invest in the financial markets, and to become *neurologically ripped*:

The simple process of focusing on the breath in a relaxed manner, in a way that teaches you to regulate your emotions by raising one's awareness of mental processes as they are happening, is like working out a bicep, but you are doing it in your brain.

Fadel Zeidan, University of North California

There has been massive interest in the human brain over recent years, with an explosion of neuroscience research – in fact, so much so that the United Nations declared the 1990s to be *"The*

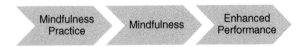

Figure 2.1 Mindfulness is the outcome of mindfulness practice.

decade of the brain". One of the most significant neuroscience findings – and one that is absolutely fundamental to this book, to me as a coach and to yourself as a trader and mindfulness participant – is that of neuroplasticity. "Neuroplasticity" is the term used to explain how the brain's structure can be modified through experience right through into adulthood; this is a huge shift from just over a decade ago, when brain structure was seen as being fixed from childhood. *Neuro* is for the neurons, which are the nerve cells in our brains and nervous system and *plastic* is used to explain the changeable and modifiable component. Neuroplasticity is the key principle behind Norman Doidge's excellent book *The Brain That Changes Itself*.[3] Doidge states that, *"The idea that the brain can change its own structure and function through thought and activity is, I believe, the most important alteration in our view of the brain since we first sketched out its basic anatomy and the workings of its basic component, the neuron"*. Within the book Doidge shares stories of a scientist who enabled a person who was blind from birth to see again, and another who enabled a deaf person to hear; there are examples of people who were cured from strokes, increased their IQ despite having learning disorders, elderly people who were able to sharpen their memory and brain function, and people who overcame obsessions and traumas.

The two key principles of neuroplasticity are:

- Neurons that fire together, wire together.
- Neurons that fire apart, wire apart.

So, it is possible to change your brain through training; you can "rewire" your thinking processes, emotional responses and behavioural tendencies to enable you to overcome specific challenges or simply learn new ways of taking your trading to the next level.

Mindfulness Practice – Mind Fitness Training

Mindfulness is a habit, it's something the more one does, the more likely one is to be in that mode with less and less effort... It's a skill that can be learned. It's accessing something we already have. Mindfulness isn't difficult. What is difficult is remembering to be mindful.

John Teasdale, leading mindfulness researcher[4]

Mindfulness is a skill and, as Teasdale states, a habit; it is an action, and to get better at it you need to practise it. There are many ways in which you can practise your mindfulness. If you were to go on a mindfulness course then, over the course of the programme, you would be introduced to a variety of different practices. Central to your learning would be a formal sitting meditation, however you would also be taught a variety of other formal practices and, importantly, a number of informal ways in which to incorporate mindfulness into your day-to-day life.

To get you started with your own mindfulness practice, I would suggest beginning with the *"Mindfulness of Breathing"* practice. This is one of the key exercises I use with my own clients, and is outlined below. I also include some information on other forms of mindfulness practice, including mindful movement, walking and how you can utilise everyday activities to develop your mindfulness capability in a more informal way. Later in the book you will find other mindfulness practices such as the *body scan* and *urge surfing*, and at the end of the book you will find all of these practices coordinated in an 8-week *TraderMind* training programme designed to take you progressively through key practices and exercises and develop your mind fitness.

Mindfulness of Breathing

In this practice you are going to use your breath as the focus of your attention (Figure 2.2). The aim is to sit comfortably and then simply allow your attention to settle on the sensations of your breathing, following the rhythm and speed of your breath, the movements of your chest and abdomen, feeling the flow of air in and out, just noticing. When your mind wanders – as my own mindfulness teacher likes to remind me "as minds do" – just notice where it went and then *gently* bring your attention back to the breath. This process is exactly the same as I

Figure 2.2 The four stages of the *Mindfulness of Breathing* practice.

utilised with athletes in my sports psychology days to develop their attentional skills.

Using your breath as a point of focus has three distinct advantages. Firstly, it is always with you and so you can perform the practice anywhere. Secondly, your physical and emotional state will be reflected in your breathing, giving you a subtle awareness of your state, and allowing you to develop greater emotional awareness. Thirdly, you can only be breathing in this moment, in the present, and so a focus upon the breath brings you into the present.

The process of focusing on the breath, noticing when your mind wanders and bringing it back again is repeated for a period of time which could be as short as 60 seconds – if you are performing a *mindful minute*, which is a great way to centre, refocus and rebalance prior to or after a specific event, or to build your number of mindfulness minutes over the day – or could extend to 5, 10 or 20 minutes at a time in a more extended practice. In sports psychology we typically used time frames of 10 to 20 minutes with athletes for attention training and if you are a trader with a busy life and demands on your time, then committing to a daily practice of something within this region might be a great starting point. I often encourage a starting point of 3 to 5 minutes per day, building to 10 as the introductory progression for my own clients.

Mindful Movement

If you would like something a little more dynamic than sitting down, then mindful movement may be the answer. Mindfulness practice provides a useful opportunity to begin to develop a greater awareness of your mind/body connection through physical movements drawn from disciplines such as yoga and tai-chi. In my travels across the world working with traders I have seen a growing number taking up yoga as a pastime, and many have asked me whether I think this would be beneficial. My response is always "yes", in fact in some studies[5] it has been shown to be as effective as cognitive-behavioural therapy in reducing feelings of stress. Yoga is a form of mindful movement, although you don't have to do yoga to do mindful movement. Actions as simple as basic stretching-type movements, but done with full awareness, are also typical of those taught on mindfulness courses.

Practice: Mindful Movement – Arm Raising and Stretching

Warning: Before you attempt any of these mindful movement exercises please ensure that you are medically fit enough to do so. If you have any known physical problems, please consult a doctor before commencing this practice. During the practice itself, if you notice any strong feelings of pain or discomfort then it may be advisable to stop. When stretching – as you will be doing – some discomfort is normal; be careful not to push beyond the limits of your body.

1 Take a moment to find a space to stand in, with bare feet or socks, feet about hips' width apart and parallel to each other, knees unlocked.
2 Slowly raise your arms out to the side of you, paying full attention to the sensations of movement, until your hands are raised above your head.
3 At this point, continue to stretch upwards, pushing your fingertips upwards towards the sky/ceiling. Notice the sensations of stretching through your body. Notice your "soft edge" – where your body begins to feel some intensity, whilst being aware of your "hard edge" – where your body is at its limit for that moment

4 Maintain this stretch and notice what happens to your breathing. Be aware of any sensations and feelings in your body as you breathe in and out. The aim is to stay a little longer around your "soft edge".

5 When you are ready, slowly and mindfully lower your arms, noticing the changes in sensations within your body as you do.

Mindful Walking

Walking is one of the four traditional meditation postures – the others being sitting, lying and standing. Mindful walking is often used in mindfulness training alongside sitting practices, alternating from one to the other, over and over again. However, more valuable for you as a trader is the opportunity to utilise mindful walking during the trading day. When you get a chance to get away from the desk for a few minutes you can practise some mindful walking, or on the way to or back home from the office – to the station. There are often opportunities like this during the day to practise mindful walking. These mindful walks can help to provide a welcome break from the information overload that traders are subject to; coming away from the endless flow of thoughts that you have at your desk and just attending to your body's sensations, rejuvenating at the same time.

How do you do it? As you are walking, slow down and pay special attention to the physical sensations of walking – the feel of your feet where the soles meet the ground; the transfer of weight from one foot to the other. Notice the flex and tension in your legs; if you become distracted by your thoughts, simply redirect your mind back to the sensations of walking. You will probably find it useful to walk more slowly as you do this, which in itself has a relaxing effect. The benefits of walking in terms of stress reduction are well known, a mindful walk takes the experience and benefits further.

Mindfulness of Routine Activities (Mindful Living)

Mindfulness training does not need to be a formal process, it can also be incorporated into your everyday existence in a more informal way. Here are some examples:

- A mindful meal – many people eat so quickly and automatically that they hardly ever really taste what they are eating. This is very common amongst traders, who typically eat at their desks whilst paying attention to the markets. To eat mindfully, slow down and really pay attention to what you are eating; let all of your senses engage in the process – smell the food, taste the food, feel the texture and temperature of the food. Where possible, try to eat mindfully at least once per week, and try a mindful lunch away from your desk.
- A mindful beer or glass of wine – I am sure I have had far too many mindless beers; downing the bottle to keep up with friends, to finish it quickly before moving to the next bar or simply not really focusing on the beer as it automatically gets consumed while I am talking or on the rare occasion (normally after too many mindless beers) dancing. Next time you have beer or wine, drink it really slowly; notice the temperature, the smell, really taste the flavour. You will never want another mindless beer again.
- Mindful exercise – many traders I work with and know like to exercise. Exercise can become mindful when you start to pay full attention to your training experience. In sports psychology this is called "becoming associated". It might be the sensations of your muscles moving, it could be the rhythm or speed of the movement. Paying attention to your breathing is an excellent way to stay focused on the moment when exercising. The feel of the water in swimming, the sensations of racquet and ball connecting in tennis... the opportunities are numerous. As always, if you notice your mind wandering, simply bring it back to the key point of your focus.
- Routine activities like brushing your teeth, getting dressed, having a cup of tea or coffee, having a shower and so on can all become mindless and it can be useful and enjoyable on

occasions to bring some mindfulness to these moments, to step out of your automated experience and really pay attention to what you are doing.

Mindful Mowing – How One Trader Developed His Own Mind Fitness Practice

I was discussing the concept of mindfulness with a trader client of mine who then recounted how he has one task each week that he likes to see completed from start to finish without interruption – mowing the grass. He told me how he ensures his family know that he is not to be interrupted and then how he goes about slowly cutting the grass, pushing the mower up and down the lawn, taking in the smell of the fresh-cut grass, hearing the sound of the engine. A very mindful experience.

How Long Will It Take?

Once traders and fund managers start to see the potential benefits of becoming more mindful and developing their mind fitness, then the next and almost inevitable question is *"How much do I have to do?"* or *"How long will it take?"* These questions are not surprising based on the already overloaded working days of traders, many of whom are now in situations where they are being expected to make their budgets but with fewer resources, and when motivation is looked at in terms of *how much effort, over what time period, for what reward.* The rewards of cultivating greater mindfulness are obvious from the research presented so far in this book, and so, of course, it comes down to how much you want those benefits and the time and effort you are willing to put into achieving them.

The component of effort is really not such a key factor, as mindfulness itself does not require significant effort in terms of workload – although it is important to re-emphasise here that mindfulness is not a passive relaxation state, but is rather a state of focus and attention, where there is some cognitive load. Time really becomes the key determinant of whether traders undertake mind fitness training, and this is common across populations who have attended mindfulness-based training. One of the biggest challenges facing mindfulness teachers is helping their students to establish a regular mindfulness practice. Considerations such as the best time of day and location are useful to note when planning your own practice. For many of my London-based traders, the commute to work provides an ideal time for mindfulness practice. For others it might be first thing in the morning, their lunch break or in the evening.

Many of the studies into the effectiveness of mindfulness training are conducted whilst people are completing the 8-week MBSR programme or its equivalents. These programmes last 8 weeks and typically have 2 hours of instruction each week and encourage 20 minutes plus home practice each day. For traders who are really curious and committed to developing their mindfulness skills, I would highly recommend a longer mindfulness programme such as the *TraderMind* one presented in this book or a local MBSR programme. One of my clients, who had attended some shorter introductory sessions I presented on developing mindfulness to enhance trading performance, went on an MBSR course in his local area and on completion of the course sent me an email, of which part read as follows:

I have just finished the MBSR program after 8 weeks and I enjoyed it.

I believed that it could be just useful techniques that I could use when stress is rising. But it's much more than that.

First I am surprised that it gives you energy, a lot of it. And it's surely better to do it in the morning than in the evening. Secondly, as I do it 30 [min] on average every day, it's very good to appreciate your breath, your thoughts, feelings… and to be in the present.

For trading, I think it's just unbelievable how it helps you to stay here and not to think about past or future.

As physical training or good nutrition, mindfulness is a good way to train your mental part. And 30 [min] per day is not too much as benefits are clearly identified.

I am sure that now mindfulness is integrated in my global trading process and is part of the whole preparation process.

And without thinking about all the other benefits you get in your life (like when playing with your children on a Sunday afternoon!)

I remember reading of a concept presented by Tim Ferris in his book *The Four Hour Body*,[6] called minimum effective dose (MED) – that is, the least I have to do to get the most effective return. This is, in some ways, not a very mindful approach, but in reality for traders and fund managers and all those involved in the financial markets where time is short, pressures are high and many also have demands and stresses outside work, it is a key question.

Mindfulness benefits can, however, be evidenced even within a short period of time. A study of 80 undergraduates from the Dalian University, headed by Professor Yi-Yuan Tang,[7] had students practise meditation for 20 minutes a day for 5 days. At the end of the 5 days the meditation group demonstrated a better attentional ability and had lower levels of cortisol (the stress hormone) than a comparative group who had been practising relaxation skills.

In another study,[8] neuroscientists found that after just five 20-minute sessions of a mindfulness meditation technique, people had increased blood flow to an area of the brain vital to self-control, the anterior cingulate cortex. After 11 hours of practice, they found actual physical changes in the brain around this area.

Research by Mark Fenton-O'Creevy *et al.* utilising mindfulness-based approaches with traders found that *"Even brief interventions can successfully induce a mindful state, improve attention, increase capacity to monitor financial information, and improve financial decision-making".*[9]

The "mind fitness" study led by Jha and Stanley had the US Marines focus on 12 minutes of practice per day. Andy Puddicombe, author of *Headspace: Ten Minutes a Day Can Make All the Difference*,[10] has a vision to get everyone taking 10 minutes of "headspace" per day. Jon Kabat-Zinn, in a presentation to employees at Google, suggested that as little as 5 minutes of mindfulness at the start of the day could be significant. *"Our studies show that a short training program in mindfulness meditation has demonstrable effects on brain and immune function"*, states Professor Richard Davidson of the University of Wisconsin.[11]

The bottom line is that something is definitely better than nothing. I have found that most of my own clients have been able to commit to 10 minutes per day, and this has brought positive effects for them. Some have gone on and started longer practices, even if infrequently, whilst others have taken a more informal route to their use of mindfulness – incorporating the use of the mindful minute, habit releasers, managing their thoughts and emotional regulation strategies as required.

Turbocharge Your Mind Fitness Development

Two key ingredients to successful learning are practice and feedback. K. Anders Ericsson, in his book *The Road to Excellence*,[12] identified a key accelerator of performance as being deliberate practice – a three-stage process of having a focus for the practice, doing the practice and then evaluating what had happened and taking action for the future based on this.

To optimise your training and increase the benefits you get from the time that you are committed, utilising such a three-stage process is essential. The three stages in the *TraderMind* mindfulness training approach are intention, practice and inquiry (Figure 2.3).

Figure 2.3 The deliberate practice learning loop for *TraderMind* mindfulness training.

Intention

In your mindfulness practice it is important to remind yourself of your intention each time that you practise – ask yourself *"What is the purpose of this practice and my mindfulness training?"*

Practice

Give your best effort to the practice. There is no standard to achieve or level of competence to work to. Whatever your experience is, that is what it is. There is always something useful that comes from it. It doesn't matter whether your mind wanders once, 10 times or 100 times.

Inquiry

The inquiry stage is the feedback part of the process, and is a key feature of mindfulness training. A good process to use for your own inquiry post-training is to follow the four steps in Figure 2.4 based on Kolb's *Model of Learning*.[13] Following the practice, reflect on your experience in terms of the feelings, thoughts and sensations that you experienced. This is purely about describing your experience, and at this stage there is no attempt to analyse or understand why you felt or thought a certain way. The next stage is to begin to relate your experience from the practice to what might be relevant within a trading (or life) context: *"What might this mean for me?"* Finally, feedforward, considering how this might apply to your future experiences: *"What does this mean for me going forward?"*

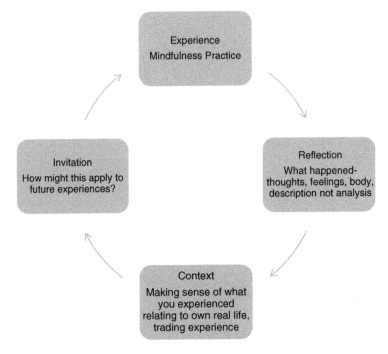

Figure 2.4 Kolb's *Model of Learning* (adapted) from mindfulness-based cognitive therapy.

Practicalities FAQ

Here are a few answers to five of the most popular questions I get asked once people are fired up and looking to start their mindfulness practice.

When is the best time of day to practise?

The best time to practise is the time at which you are most likely to be able to do so. Many people choose to do their practice early in the morning, and if they are doing two sessions in a day then again in the evening. Practising shortly before you start trading can be very helpful in preparing your mind and body for trading and creating the relaxed alertness that is so beneficial for traders; carrying that mindset into the trading day. If lunchtime is better for you, do it at lunchtime. Some of my clients use their tube or train journeys for their mind fitness training time. The key is to find the time that works for you. Finding a regular time so that you can *build in* rather than *fit in* your practice is a good way of looking at it.

What do I need to wear?

There is no specific type of clothing required for you to practise in, although generally, relaxed, loose clothing may be more comfortable.

Where is the best place to practise?

Generally, somewhere comfortable and quiet where you won't get interrupted is a good place for your formal practice; however, I encourage my clients to be more flexible in their approach. Practise wherever you are when you have the time to do so – except when driving or doing any other kind of hazardous pursuit. You can practise at home, in the office, in the garden, in the park, on the train – wherever you feel comfortable and can maintain the required level of concentration. For me personally, any opportunity to practise outside in nature is always taken and one of my favourite mindfulness group sessions was conducted with a group of traders at the end of the trading day in a beautiful park close to their office, with the sun shining.

How long should I practise for?

How long you practise for is going to depend to some degree on the time you have available, how committed you are to your training and the actual practice you are doing. Initially, I always advise my clients to start their practice with 3 to 5 minutes per day. If they feel they would like to do more, then 5 minutes twice a day is a good next step. The aim is to establish regular practice. As time progresses you can gradually increase from 5 minutes up to 10 minutes and then beyond towards 15-, 20-, 30- or even 45-minute time frames should you wish. Remember, even when time is really short you should be able to conduct a short practice. In *TraderMind* there are some practices as short as 1 or 3 minutes long; some days you may not be able to get a longer practice in but may find yourself more able to fit in two or three short sessions over the course of the day.

What equipment do I need?

No specific equipment is required; a comfortable chair and an open mind. Some people like to listen to guided mind fitness practices, and so in this case your recordings, an audio player and either speakers or headphones will be necessary.

You Have To Do Your Own Press-Ups

Like most activities, you only get out what you put in and so the more time you spend practising mindfulness the quicker you will notice the benefits and the greater they will be. Jon Kabat-Zinn, in his book *Full Catastrophe Living*, raises the notion of intention – the intention to maintain your mindfulness practice, whether you feel like it or not, with the determination of an athlete.

The formal mindfulness practices presented in this book are all designed to take 10 minutes or less. This works really well based on the research, but also from my experience of using mindfulness-based training with traders. It makes it manageable and achievable for anyone who is interested and committed to training their mind and enhancing their performance. Of course, like anything, there are limitations to this approach, and if you have (or can find) more time then participating in some longer mind fitness sessions will reap additional benefits. Maybe try a full 8-week programme or try a yoga class. Ideally, make mindfulness part of your lifestyle.

Intention is one of the three components of a model for mindfulness proposed by Shapiro *et al.*,[14] the other two being attention and attitude (Figure 2.5). Attitude is a key part of mind fitness training. Commitment, curiosity, compassion and patience are all key attitudes for cultivating mindfulness. *"The spirit in which you do something is often as important as the act itself"*, as Mark Williams tells us in his book.

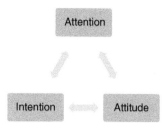

Figure 2.5 The three axioms of intention, attention and attitude (IAA).

To finish the chapter I would like to return to the quote by John Teasdale: *"Mindfulness is a habit, it's something the more one does, the more likely one is to be in that mode with less and less effort... It's a skill that can be learned. It's accessing something we already have. Mindfulness isn't difficult. What is difficult is remembering to be mindful."*

3

The Attention and Awareness Advantage

Awareness, Attention and Automatic Pilot

From Socrates to the boom of the self-help era, the concept of self-awareness, represented by the maxim "Know Thyself", has been promoted as a key principle to being happier, healthier and wealthier, and to performing at a higher level. You will see references to the importance of self-awareness in philosophy, psychology, leadership, learning, trading, sports and self-improvement. In his book *Self Awareness – The Hidden Driver of Success and Satisfaction*, Travis Bradberry shares findings from his research across occupations that 83% of those people with high scores for self-awareness were top performers, with just 2% of bottom performers scoring high in self-awareness.[1]

So we can conclude that self-awareness is important, and that it impacts on performance. But what exactly is it? Dr Kevin Oschner, Head of the Social Cognitive Neuroscience Laboratory, Columbia University, New York, explains it like this: *"Self-awareness is the capacity to step outside your own skin and look at yourself with as close to an objective eye as is possible."*[2] This ability to *step outside yourself*, to observe your own experience, has been likened by neuroscientists to having an *impartial spectator*, which ties in very well with the "non-judgemental" aspect of being mindful. A study in the *Journal Perspectives on Psychological*

Science,[3] for example, showed that mindfulness can help you to overcome your "blind spots" and see yourself more objectively, to increase your self-awareness.

Former fund manager Tom Basso provides an interesting insight into his own self-awareness in Van K. Tharp's book *Super Trader*:[4]

In situations where I felt I needed improvement or in which I wanted to improve my interactions with other people, I would just play key events back in my head – figuring out how others had handled the situation... I've always thought of it as some Tom Basso up in the corner of the room watching Tom Basso here talking to you in the room. The funny thing about this secondary observer was that as time went on, I found the observer showing up a lot more. It wasn't just at the end of the day anymore. As I got into stressful situations, as I started trading, doing more interacting with a lot of people, getting our business off the ground, dealing with clients, and so on. I found that this observer was there to help me through it. If I felt awkward or uneasy, then I was able to watch myself do it. Now I have this observer there all the time.

So being able to objectively reflect on and monitor your own trading experience – to be an observer of yourself – is how self-awareness could be seen as a trading quality; but why is it important? What benefits does it provide? Well, without self-awareness it would be very difficult to moderate and direct your behaviour. Self-awareness enables you to step outside the automatic flow of experience that we all encounter, and to access choice and flexibility over where you direct your attention and energy, to regulate your thoughts, feelings and behaviours. Ex-racing driver turned coach John Whitmore, in his best-selling book *Coaching for Performance*,[5] sees it like this: "*I am able to control only that of which I am aware. That of which I am unaware controls me.*"

The research, as we have seen in Chapter 1, shows that people who are more mindful are more aware of their thoughts, emotions, feelings and behaviours and as a result are better able to manage them. The process of paying attention to your experience in the present moment on purpose, which is core to

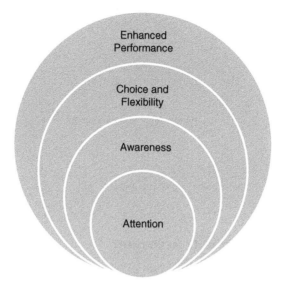

Figure 3.1 Attention builds awareness, which leads to choice and flexibility and enhanced performance.

mindfulness, builds your awareness (Figure 3.1). The more time you spend noticing, the more your awareness builds, and awareness leads to choice and flexibility, which are key to achieving your best trading performance. One of the primary reasons for developing your mindful awareness is to raise your level of self-awareness to the point where you can begin to notice your experience in real time, recognising in that moment the impact of your thoughts and emotions, noticing any impulses or urges that you may have and being aware of any habits that may be at play. Michael Chaskalson[6] puts this as: "*On automatic pilot we miss things, and some of what we miss might have a significant impact on your performance. The capacity to come out of automatic pilot a bit more often, to place your attention where you want it to be and to keep it there for longer is a known outcome of mindfulness training.*"

Mindfulness is about paying attention to yourself, others and the world around you, so there are three dimensions to your awareness (Figure 3.2). This means that mindfulness can offer much more than just self-awareness; it also has the ability to develop your situational awareness and your market awareness.

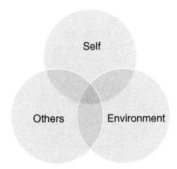

Figure 3.2 The three dimensions of awareness.

Awareness of Self: Accessing Choice and Flexibility

In a car you can sometimes drive for miles on *automatic pilot* with a very low conscious awareness of what you are doing, and in the same way you may experience this in your trading. I know of some day traders in proprietary trading groups, for example, who find themselves coming in day after day in a quite mindless pattern of behaviour with low levels of focus and awareness – this is not a good place to be. When you are in automatic pilot mode you are more likely to react to triggers of old habits, ways of thinking and feeling. With a greater awareness of thoughts, feelings, bodily sensations, from moment to moment you have a greater possibility of freedom and choice, and can respond to situations with choice rather than reacting automatically to the same mental and emotional ruts of the past. This ability is explained eloquently by Daniel Siegel of the Mindful Awareness Research Center UCLA in David Rock's book *Your Brain At Work:*[2] "*It's our ability to pause before we react... it gives us the space of mind in which we can consider various options and then choose the most appropriate ones... with the acquisition of a stabilised and refined focus on the mind itself, previously undifferentiated pathways of firing become detectable and then accessible to modification, it is in this way that we can use the mind to change the function and ultimately the structure of the brain.*" This ability to *pause before we react* is key to self-regulation and

Figure 3.3 Mindless reacting.

self-control, or as we might call it in trading terms – discipline. Studies[7] conducted by neuroscientists found that an area of the brain known as the right ventrolateral prefrontal cortex (RVLPFC) is associated with self-control. The research team found that people with greater self-control (a higher level of RVLPFC activation) were more able to resist the effect of what is known as inter-temporal discounting – a tendency in us to value money in the present more strongly than money in the future; for example, taking the offer of $100 now, rather than waiting for $110 next week, or in trading terms taking profits early. This area of brain activation was found to be greater in people with higher dispositional mindfulness – they had a greater capacity for self-control. In neuroscience this capacity to overcome such urges and temptations, to fend off the desire for instant gratification, to offset potential pleasure from the present to the future, is often called "inhibition" or "veto power". When you are in profit in a trade and get that anxious feeling and an urge to exit early, it is this process of inhibition that can keep you in, likewise with taking a loss, taking a trade following a previous loss or resisting the impulse to trade to relieve boredom.

With heightened mindful awareness you can move from a stimulus–react pattern of automaticity (Figure 3.3) to a stimulus–pause–respond pattern of choice and flexibility (Figure 3.4).

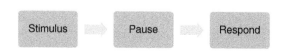

Figure 3.4 Mindful responding.

Awareness of the Environment: Situational Awareness

So far we have mainly considered awareness at an internal, "self" level, as an ability to notice thoughts, emotions, bodily sensations, urges and impulses. However, there is another dimension to awareness, and that is an external awareness – what is known in the military as *situational awareness*. Situational awareness is a key ability for decision makers in complex, dynamic areas including fighter pilots, air traffic controllers, ship navigation, the military and in rapid response emergency services such as firefighting and policing. I believe that it is also highly important to decision making in the financial markets, a complex and dynamic risk environment.

Situational awareness is the ability to be aware of what is going on around you, to be able to assess and absorb information from the external environment effectively, and respond to it most appropriately.

The most common theoretical framework of situational awareness is provided by Mica Endsley,[8] whose model illustrates three stages or steps of situational awareness formation: perception, comprehension and projection.

Perception

This is a trader's ability to notice what is happening around him from an awareness of price movements on screens, observing chart patterns, taking in and absorbing news flow from screens and squawk systems, as well as sensing changes in behaviour and mood on the trading floor.

Comprehension

The next stage in situational awareness is where traders make sense of their observations, creating a "picture" of the markets through the processes of pattern recognition, interpretation and evaluation.

Projection

The third stage of situational awareness is being able to project what is known about the situation into future actions, considering the current situation and making future predictions of what might happen.

Mindfulness develops your ability to notice what is happening around you, to be more attentive and alert to environmental cues, to increase your "feel", to become more situationally aware. It also plays a part in helping to reduce the impact of those heavily biased perceptual filters, attentional drivers and habitual tendencies you may have at the perception stage. Mindfulness, as we saw from the studies with the US Marines, also helps your situational awareness by increasing your working memory capacity under stress. Working memory is required in the situational awareness process, and in choosing the appropriate response. Experienced traders may have an advantage over newer traders in this respect in that well-formed mental models and pattern recognition developed over the years may help to offset any degradation in working memory capacity. Situational awareness plus behavioural flexibility is key to optimum trading and investing decision making.

Awareness of Others: Sentiment and the Empathy Edge

The third dimension of awareness is awareness of others. In trading and investing this awareness can be translated into an awareness of other market participants – having a feel for the market and being aware of the sentiment. This ability is related to empathy and *theory of mind* (the ability of one person to understand the thoughts, feelings and behaviours of another) and helps traders to make more effective decisions by having a greater awareness of the context of the market as a whole, rather than just the single focus of their own trading or investing strategy. Even with increasing automation in the markets, there is still a large underlying human factor, and traders and fund managers who are able to tap into that through their awareness and feel, and add it into their decision framework or process, may well create an additional edge for themselves in the markets. In *More Money Than God*,[9] legendary trader Paul Tudor-Jones is described as a trader with high empathy, who was really able to understand the other people in the market, get a feel for how they were feeling, and adopt those perspectives and insights in his trading decisions.

A study performed with surgeons in the USA,[10] which taught them key mindfulness skills, found that compared with a control group, the surgeons who underwent the training made fewer mistakes in surgery but were very interestingly also rated higher by their patients for patient care. The most likely explanation for this is that through their mindfulness practice they developed greater awareness of themselves, and others, and were better able to empathise and connect with their patients, and exhibit a better bedside manner even if they were not doing it consciously. As a trader or fund manager the practice of mindfulness will enable you to gain greater awareness and insights into your thinking, feeling and behaviour, and as you become more skilful at having an awareness and understanding of yourself, you will find that you also become more able to get in tune with the thinking, feeling and behaviour of others. You will have developed a greater *theory of mind* and be able to be more empathetic. You will have developed an *empathy edge*.

Attention, Attention, Attention

Being able to focus, to pay attention, is a key performance skill whether you are a trader, athlete, musician, surgeon or pilot. Attention plays a key role in trading performance and decision making. Where you place your attention influences your thoughts, emotions, feelings and behaviours and impacts on the brain pathways that are used, formed and strengthened. *Where attention goes, energy flows* (Figure 3.5). In his book *The Attention Revolution*,[11] B. Alan Wallace states that: *"Few things affect our lives more than the faculty of attention. If we can't focus our attention – we*

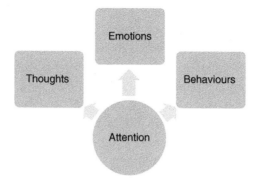

Figure 3.5 Where attention goes, energy flows.

can't do anything well." Attention is also, as we saw earlier in this chapter, key to the development of awareness.

Mindfulness training improves your attentional abilities, as highlighted in Chapter 1, by increasing:

- The ability to sustain your attention for longer.
- The ability to notice when you have become distracted more quickly.
- The ability to refocus more quickly.

The practice of focusing your attention on your breath, body or other stimuli for long periods of time transfers over to your trading as the changes that occur in your brain through mindfulness practice become available for you during your trading and investing.[12] The brain that practises mindfulness is the brain that trades the markets; just as going to the gym and lifting weights builds strength in your muscles that is then available for carrying the shopping, playing sports or moving furniture outside of the gym.

Trading in the Zone

One of the key topics that is often mentioned in trading is that of *"trading in the zone"*; getting into that state where you are fully engaged in an almost effortless performance, making good decisions, trading at your best. Maybe you have had such an experience yourself. One of the key components in achieving flow is a capacity to access the present moment, where high performance happens, and this concept – of being in the present – is at the root of mindfulness. By developing your mindfulness ability you are also developing your ability to be in the present moment more often, to be able to more easily enter that fully immersed zone state. This has particularly high relevance for shorter time frame traders who will benefit from entering this level of immersion into the market, being with the market moment to moment, feeling it, reading it and responding to it.

From another perspective, this ability to keep more of a present moment focus can be very helpful in managing the tendency for the thinking mind to ruminate and deliberate over past events, or worry about future ones. The mind has a strong tendency to wander to the past and to the future, and mindfulness training can help to develop your ability both to notice this and bring it back to the present where appropriate and useful.

For trading, I think it is just unbelievable how mindfulness helps you to stay here and not to think about the past or future.
Energy trader after mindfulness-based coaching

One of the key distinctions in making good trading decisions is noticing whether your attention is on your P&L (results) or whether it is on your trading process, making the best decision possible in the context that you are in. Where traders focus too much on P&L they are prone to decision errors which come from the underlying thinking processes and emotional responses – such as anxiety – that are triggered. Thinking about your P&L *per se* is not harmful, but at times when you really want to make a trading decision, the more you can focus on your trading process – noticing what the market is doing and staying in contact with your decision process, such as entry criteria and signals, management of your positions and your exit criteria – then the better your decisions will be, and ultimately the greater your returns from the market.

One FX trader I coached at an investment bank was able to make a significant shift in his trading performance by focusing more on his trading process, how he was making or losing money, and less on the results, how much he was making or losing. A combination of some short mindfulness-based practices with a daily decision process evaluation helped to keep his mind focused on the right cues. Traders and fund managers should focus their attention on the factors that matter, on developing an effective decision-making process. Excessive focus on specific trading and investment outcomes is likely to increase the risk of performance anxiety and choking, a failure to perform, as is seen often in sports. Practising mindfulness, developing your attention, can therefore help you to perform more effectively under pressure by keeping your focus in the present, and on task-relevant cues. As Warren Buffett says, *"We enjoy the process far more than the proceeds"*.

Attention Deficit Trait

One final note that should be of interest to traders is the effect of the trading environment on the brain's attentional abilities. The development of technology and 24/7 communication, the amounts of information that traders are exposed to each day via email, squawk, television, instant messenger and phone, the flickering of lights and numbers, all create a vibrant and stimulating environment for the brain, but ultimately one that could potentially have some detrimental effects. An article published in *The Harvard Business Review: On Point*, entitled "Overloaded circuits: Why smart people underperform",[13] reports on a neurological phenomenon called attention deficit trait (ADT). ADT is marked by distractibility and impatience. It isn't an illness or genetic medical condition such as attention deficit disorder (ADD), but is the result of exposure to the extremely high amounts of stimulation and information overload that are prevalent in the modern workplace, and the trading floor would be at the extreme of this. In this article the author suggests sleep, exercise and nutrition as key parts of keeping a healthy brain and warding off the effects of ADT, he also states the importance of accessing *positive* emotions. When you practise mindfulness you activate your left prefrontal cortex, the part of your brain that is concerned with positive emotions; you also bring your brain to a point of singular focus, which is a very different experience from the multiple sensory stimulation of the trading floor. The combination of bringing your brain back to basics with mindfulness and the positive emotions experienced as a result could be key to fending off the distractibility and impatience that ADT can bring.

Being able to focus and resist distraction, having a strong faculty of attention, is also linked to your ability to control your impulses, emotions and achieve your goals. Studies with children[14,15] have found that those with greater attentional skills and the ability to regulate their impulses are:

- Four times less likely to have a criminal record.
- Three times less likely to be addicted to drugs.
- Have more satisfying marriages.
- Have lower body mass index.

Over $3 billion a year is being spent on "smart drugs" to enhance attention. Mindfulness training is the natural way to develop greater focus and concentration, and enhance your trading performance.

Training Your Attention and Awareness: Building Metacognitive Muscle

The process of awareness and attention control is known as "metacognition". Through the seemingly simple process of paying attention to a part of your experience in the moment, whilst also noticing when your mind wanders from this point of attention, you are developing the four key processes of meta-cognitive awareness, at the same time creating a stability of the mind that will enable you to more effectively notice and be open to your present-moment experience.

A simple way of developing attention regulation is through what is known as a *focused attention* practice, where you place your attention on a single object and, when you notice that your mind has wandered, you acknowledge it and then return it back to the chosen object. This practice is quite common in sports psychology, with athletes using objects such as balls as a focus of attention. A typical mindfulness practice might utilise your breathing as the object of attention:

Focus your entire attention on your incoming and outgoing breath. Try to sustain your attention there without distraction. If you get distracted, calmly return your attention to the breath and start again.

Training in such ways enables you to extend your concentration, get distracted less and recover from distractions more quickly – all of which are key performance skills. The ability to concentrate on your breath, or an object, whilst being aware of and disregarding distractions is known as "conflict monitoring" or "executive attention" and is a key process in developing the ability to regulate your thoughts, emotions and bodily sensations more effectively. At brain level it is the anterior cingulate cortex (ACC) that is responsible for this executive attention process. It is also important here to stress that developing sufficient levels of attention is required to enable you to stay engaged in your mindfulness practices and stop you drifting off and daydreaming.

Try this simple *Mindfulness of Breathing* practice to experience the four metacognitive processes in action.

Practice: Mindfulness of Breathing

Start by sitting comfortably in an upright position.

- Close your eyes if you feel comfortable doing so, otherwise maintain a loose gaze towards the floor.
- Focus your attention on one of your more prominent sensations of breathing – it could be the speed or rhythm, the feeling of your chest or diaphragm rising and falling, or the flow of air around the nostrils, for example.
- When you notice that your attention has drifted, and it will – usually quite quickly – bring it back to the sensations of breathing.
- These attentional shifts – mind wandering – are normal, it is what minds do. Recognising that the mind has wandered is a part of mindfulness training. No matter how many times your mind wanders, simply bring it back to the breath.
- Stay with this for about 3–5 minutes.

In doing that practice you are experiencing, and training, the four metacognitive skills:

1 The skill of placing the mind where you want it to be (*I will focus on the sensation of my breath*).
2 The skill of keeping the mind where you want it to be (*I will keep my attention on my breathing*).
3 The skill of sensing when your mind is not where you want it to be (*I focus on my breathing but notice when my mind wanders*).
4 The skill of detaching the mind from where you don't want it to be (*I realise I do not want my mind to be where it has wandered to, and I refocus on the sensations of breathing*).

By practising these skills you become better at them, developing the awareness and attentional capabilities that will enable you to become better at managing your trading internal experience and developing your brain in such a way that you are less reactive, more responsive and a more effective decision maker.

One commodities trader who completed a course on trading using mindfulness-based approaches was able to identify a key shift in his perspective: *"When I am trading it is like I am watching from outside myself, a 3rd person perspective."* Another trader noted: *"Since practising the mindfulness exercises I have become more attentive both in and out of trading."* Metacognition is a skill and it can be trained with noticeable and beneficial results.

Applied Metacognition

In this chapter we have looked at the importance of awareness and attention – how to develop your metacognitive capabilities – and considered the role of attention in trading performance. These ideas and practices alone are powerful and can create significant shifts in your performance potential however, the goal is now to take your metacognitive capabilities and apply them to help you manage your thinking, emotions, feelings and behaviours so that you can enhance your trading decision making and performance.

4

Thinking About Thinking

Thinking About Markets and Trading

Put this book to one side. Take a moment to sit, close your eyes and let your mind calm, and let all of your thoughts stop for just a few minutes.

How did it go? It is highly likely that you found your mind was far from quiet, and you probably experienced more of what is known as "monkey mind", with thoughts of all types coming and going.

Traders spend a great deal of time thinking about the markets, their positions, trading, other traders and themselves, and their experiences as traders. What you think about, perceive and believe about the markets, other traders, the world, risk, uncertainty, winning, losing and yourself ultimately influences the decisions you make as a trader and the results that you get – they are filters of your experience, as shown in Figure 4.1. As Van K. Tharp, author of *Trade Your Way to Financial Freedom*[1] puts it: *"You do not trade the markets, you trade your beliefs about the markets."* Thoughts and beliefs as simple as *the market is going up* can have a profound impact on your behaviour and decision making. Sometimes these thoughts will be useful and helpful to you, at other times they will hinder you, clouding your judgement and swaying your actions. A large part of your thinking activity occurs outside

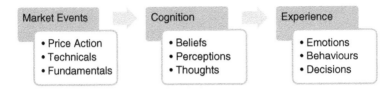

Market Events	Cognition	Experience
• Price Action • Technicals • Fundamentals	• Beliefs • Perceptions • Thoughts	• Emotions • Behaviours • Decisions

Figure 4.1 The effect of cognition on your trading experience.

your conscious awareness, but you will also be able to recall times when a particular train of thought, a strongly held view or a perception about the market came to your conscious awareness, sat in your mind and influenced your emotions, feelings and actions.

Becoming more mindful, having a greater awareness of your thoughts, beliefs and perceptions, and learning to relate to them in a different way, with less attachment, can help you to enhance your trading decisions.

Cognitive Awareness

One of the central processes of mindfulness training is that of developing your awareness and attention, because, as we have already discovered, that is central to being able to manage your internal experience, and therefore your thoughts, more effectively. The first step in working more effectively with your thoughts, beliefs and perceptions is developing a greater awareness of them, and this can be done in a number of ways.

Here is a very effective exercise that you can do to start to develop your present-moment cognitive awareness.

Practice: Thought Awareness

- Close your eyes and simply notice what your mind does. Stay on the lookout for any thoughts or images. If no thoughts or images appear, just keep watching.
- Notice where your thoughts seem to be located – in front of you, above you, behind you, to one side of you, within you. Notice the tone of the thoughts and whether there are any images present or not.
- Notice that part of you is thinking, while another part of you is observing you thinking.

This exercise encourages you to start noticing and observing your thoughts, but also, and very importantly, it enables you to start making the distinction between you being your thoughts, attached and as one, versus you observing your thoughts, with thoughts now being perceived as mental events of the mind. This step towards seeing thoughts as mental events already allows you to experience your thoughts very differently, to relate to them in a different way and to work with them more effectively. Thoughts are mental events, they are not you and they are not facts. We cannot always choose the thoughts that pop into our mind, but we can choose how much attention we give them.

Some useful metaphors for observing thoughts include imagining thoughts as leaves on a stream with you watching from the river bank, or as trains on a series of tracks with you on the platform, or as traffic on the road with you watching from the side. Whatever the metaphor, and maybe one of those is useful for you or maybe you can think of your own, the concept is the same – that we are the observers of our thoughts and not those thoughts themselves. This was an important distinction and a key insight for one trader I worked with at an energy company, who was under a lot of pressure and stress following an unusually long period of low returns from the market; in fact his first real period of drawdown in his career; combined with the birth of his first child and a subsequent lack of sleep. As time went on he found himself becoming more and more negative in his thinking, and the feelings and emotions that were sitting alongside these thoughts and perceptions were leading to behaviours that were not conducive to optimal trading performance within the context he was in. He was becoming more and more risk averse and with lower energy levels was becoming less able to engage fully in his role and with the markets. He was underperforming not just in P&L terms but importantly, behaviourally. His thinking was a major source of interference to him taking effective trading action. Following the exercise you completed above, he found that the idea of seeing thoughts on train carriages and being able to watch them from the platform provided him with a different perspective on those thoughts, with a lower level of intensity and frustration arising from them. The thoughts were the same, yet his experience of them was different. Just having a greater awareness of your thoughts alone can be very powerful in enhancing your trading behaviour.

An excellent way of developing your thought awareness is through the *Mindfulness of Sounds and Thoughts* practice presented below. We are in a world of almost constant noise, sounds come and go, get louder and quieter, some stay around for a while, some come and go more quickly. Sounds can also trigger reactions and emotions, some of which can be powerful. This practice reveals the similarity between sounds and thoughts, in that both sounds and thoughts can appear almost as if from nowhere; they can be quite random, yet have a strong power to influence our emotional and behavioural responses. This practice will help you to develop a greater awareness of your thoughts whilst at the same time helping you to develop a different relationship with your thoughts. One fund manager that I introduced mindfulness to with a brief mindfulness of breathing exercise found that his mind wandered incessantly and randomly, and I remember him telling me in a state of curious wonderment: *"I started thinking about USB data storage – and I don't ever think about that."* The mind wanders, it is what minds do. In fact, this is a good place to stress that mindfulness practice is not about clearing the mind of thoughts. Rather, it is about having an awareness of those thoughts, being able to see them as thoughts, as mental events and being able to exercise choice and flexibility in which ones you choose to focus on and act upon.

Practice: Mindfulness of Sounds and Thoughts

Settling into the Practice
- Find a comfortable, upright seated position, back supported, shoulders relaxed.
- Bring your attention to your breathing for a few minutes, before expanding your attention to your body as a whole.

Sounds
- Allow the focus of your attention to shift to sounds.
- There is no need to go searching for sounds. Just stay open and receptive to sounds. Noticing sounds as they arise.
- As best you can, be aware of sounds simply as sounds. Noticing as you do this our tendency to label sounds (car, air conditioning, radio).
- Whenever you find that your attention has drifted away from sounds, simply acknowledge where it has gone to, and then refocus back onto sounds.

Thoughts
- Now shift your awareness to thoughts.
- Just like with sounds there is no need to go searching for thoughts. Simply notice them as they arise, linger and dissolve.
- Some people like to notice their thoughts as clouds in the sky, leaves on a stream or words on a cinema-type screen.
- You might like to notice any emotional reactions that come with your thoughts, and how you react to them.
- If at any time you feel yourself getting drawn into your thinking, simply bring your attention back to your breathing.

Closing
- When you are ready, simply bring attention back to your breath.
- Then close the practice by bringing full attention back to the room.

Another way that you can develop a greater awareness of your thoughts, beliefs and perceptions is to consciously identify them using the *Identifying Beliefs and Perceptions* exercise below. Here you can start to uncover some of your key thoughts and perceptions about the markets, trading, yourself and others by completing the sentence starters. The longer you give yourself to complete the exercise, generally the deeper and more valuable the cognitions that you uncover will be. Simply having an awareness of these thoughts, beliefs and perceptions is enough to start reducing their influence, and the likelihood that you will act on them. Awareness reduces reactivity.

Practice: Identifying Beliefs and Perceptions

- Take a moment to sit and reflect on your trading.
- As you sit quietly, bring to mind the key thoughts and stories you tell yourself about yourself, trading, the markets, other traders, the world. "I am/I am not..." "Markets are/are not..." "Trading is/is not..." "They are/are not..." "It is/is not..." "Losing is/is not..." "Winning is/is not..." "Risk is/is not..." "Uncertainty is/is not..." "Success is/is not..." "Money is/is not..."
- After you begin to identify these beliefs, begin to inquire closely. Are these beliefs useful? Are they helping you to achieve what you want in your trading? Are they getting in the way of you achieving what you want from your trading?

You may find it helpful, following this practice, to take a few moments to write down what you discovered. Also, repeating the practice for a period of time will allow you to reveal some of your more deeply held beliefs and perceptions.

With many of my clients I have encouraged them, at the start of each day, to take a few minutes to write down their key thoughts, beliefs and perceptions about the markets, trading and themselves, alongside how they are feeling. This is a way of bringing to conscious awareness their current *"internal context"*, and in doing so reducing any possible unhelpful influence of their thoughts and feelings on their trading decisions. One trader utilising this methodology reported how *"One of the approaches that I have implemented from the coaching sessions that has had the biggest impact on my trading has been the simple act of writing down my thoughts and market perceptions at the start of the day. It helped to clarify my thinking and give me a better awareness of my current views and potential biases."*

Simply having an awareness of your thoughts, beliefs and perceptions can change your decision making and behaviour. This is one of the key facets of mindfulness-based approaches, and the goal is not so much to change or control the thought – as is common in many cognitive-based psychologies – but rather to change the way in which you relate to your thoughts.

How Do You Stop Thinking About a White Bear?

What I would like you to do now is to take 5 minutes, sit still and quietly, and try not to think about a white bear. Every time you catch yourself thinking about a white bear make a note, keep a score.

How did that go?

Now repeat the task again.

This task was at the heart of a study into thought suppression headed by Daniel Wegner in 1987 and written about in his book *White Bears and Other Unwanted Thoughts* published in 1992.[2] In the study conducted by Wegner and his team, people were asked not to think of a *white bear* for 5 minutes, to use suppression (blocking) to stop the thought from happening, but if they did get the thought then they had to ring a bell. Following this initial 5 minutes, participants were told not to think about the *white bear* for a further 5 minutes. Using suppression strategies to resist thinking about the white bear increased the frequency of thinking about the white bear, especially in the second stage with the people who used thought suppression on average ringing the bell about once a minute. How did you do?

There have been many subsequent experimental studies examining the impact of thought suppression which have come to similar conclusions: that suppression may not be helpful either in the present or in the short term and that, paradoxically, suppression may actually increase the number of times the thought occurs. Suppression is also metabolically demanding, it requires brain energy and so has an impact on your energy levels and – as we are braking, applying resistance – it can also, as a result of this depleting of energy, lead to an inability to exercise self-control, or discipline, in the future.

Letting Go of the Struggle

Rakesh is a trader with about 5 years' experience in the markets who has had some challenges in taking losses on his trades; one of the main factors behind this has been the amount of self-talk interference he has had from his thoughts: *"I can't get out now"* *"The market will come back"* *"You can't afford to take that loss"*. These were all thoughts that he had. Up until the point of our coaching session his strategy for dealing with these thoughts had been to try to ignore them, suppress them or reason with them. His experience had been that in the moment it was *"a battle"* between him and his thoughts, and that he was still experiencing the thoughts in future situations and was still not taking the losses. Furthermore, his experience was such that the battle was tiring for him and while he was in the battle he was not fully focused on the markets – he had lost situational awareness.

Rakesh was in a *struggle with his thoughts*. To help Rakesh move forward, I worked on helping him to relate to his thoughts differently, to give up the struggle and to be more open with and less attached to his thoughts. This involved a process of developing his awareness of his thoughts, noticing them as thoughts, looking at them in terms of utility (usefulness) and then using a strategy called cognitive defusion (explained later in this chapter) to help him manage them more effectively in the moment. This process is based on key mindfulness and acceptance principles, where we *turn towards our thoughts* rather than suppressing them or fighting against them. It is very effective for many traders in a number of different situations, as we shall explore.

Before you read any further in this chapter, take a moment to answer the question below. Your responses to it will then provide you with some thoughts, beliefs and perceptions to work with in the remaining exercises of this chapter.

What memories, worries, fears, self-criticisms or other unhelpful thoughts do you get caught up in that interfere with your trading decisions and results?

Working With Thoughts – Acceptance

We have already seen how the suppression of your thoughts is not necessarily a useful strategy for managing them; it is cognitively demanding, depletes brain energy and often leads to the same thoughts recurring in the future. The alternative is to be more open and accepting of your thoughts. From your experience of the exercises in this chapter you may already be able to get a sense that it is not the thoughts themselves that are the problem *per se*, but rather how you relate to them and importantly, how attached to them you are. Indeed, in terms of the degree of influence that your thoughts, beliefs and perceptions have over your decisions, your degree of attachment to them could be the driving factor, and it is strong attachment to market views that may reduce a trader's flexibility in their position taking – to be able to go short as the market falls following an initial long position or holding a long view. Being the observer, the impartial spectator of your thinking, creates a different emotional and behavioural perspective and experience.

When you start to view thoughts as mental events from the observer position, becoming aware of your thoughts, then you are relating to and experiencing your thoughts in a very different way, with less attachment and more flexibility. A key distinction and a key shift to make is one away from thoughts directly controlling actions – as some cognitive models may propose – to thoughts *influencing* actions.

Practice: Working With Difficult Thoughts

When you find yourself caught up in unhelpful patterns of thinking, try the following:

- Acknowledge the thoughts for what they are... thoughts. You may find it useful to put a label on them: "There's me planning, judging, criticising, worrying."

(continued)

- Just sit for a moment, noticing what is happening with your thinking.
- Now turn your attention to your body and notice what feelings and emotions are present; just notice.
- Next turn your attention to bodily sensations – tension, tightness, curiosity – and be aware of what you find. Sit for a few moments with those sensations, exploring them, breathing with them, just letting them be.

Cognitive Utility – The Lens of "Usefulness"

When we look at beliefs and thoughts we need to recognise them as mental events, but also to be mindful of them and neither take them on as true nor dismiss them as false initially. Your thoughts and mental processes can obviously be hugely helpful to you at times, however they can also become the interference that stops you from following through on effective action in your trading decision making. A good lens to observe your thoughts is that of *utility* – is this thought useful to me in the context of what I am trying to achieve, or not?

An example of this could be the trader I worked with who, 8 months into the financial year, was really struggling with his trading and as a committed professional had been putting in lots of extra hours and was really working hard to turn his performance around but was, by this time, both frustrated and exhausted. When we discussed his situation and talked about effective action, he mentioned that probably the best action would be to take a break and go on holiday. It was coming up towards August, the markets were quiet, it was a time when traditionally he had taken his holiday and he felt the break would enable him to recharge, refresh and refocus. However, even though he put a fantastic case forward for taking the break, he was not actually doing it. Why? He was attached to a belief that was not useful for him in this context. The belief was one that he had acquired from his very early years in trading from his then head of desk, who was a very committed trader himself and had a rule for the desk: *"If you are down*

P&L for the year (losing money) then you can't take a holiday." Being down P&L for this year meant that under the "rule", even though taking a break would be the most skillful and effective action, he was not doing so and was stuck. Like all beliefs and perceptions, none of them are right or wrong, but they can be viewed as either useful or not useful – especially when we also take into account the context and look at effective action in line with our goals and values as a trader.

I asked my client whether that belief was useful or not. He replied: *"Not really, not now."*

Being able to identify the utility of your thoughts, beliefs and perceptions can be useful on several levels, including simply holding that awareness, but also helping with later approaches to identify which specific thoughts and perceptions you may wish to work on.

Identifying the utility of your thoughts can be done by asking one or more of the questions below:

- Is this thought/belief in any way useful or helpful?
- Is this an old story?
- What would I get from buying into this story?
- Could this be helpful?
- Does this thought/belief help me to take effective action?
- Am I going to trust my mind or my experience?

Exercise: Utility of Thoughts, Beliefs and Perceptions

Have a look at your collection of beliefs and perceptions from earlier in the chapter. With what you are trying to achieve in your trading, classify them according to "utility" under three headings: useful, neutral, not useful.

With the beliefs that at present have little or no utility, you can practise using some of the approaches that follow in this chapter to work on them and reduce any potential "negative" impact on your trading decisions.

Utility of thoughts, beliefs and perceptions

Useful	Neutral	Not Useful

Cognitive Fusion – Attachment to Thoughts

As we have seen in this chapter, it is not necessarily the thoughts or beliefs and perceptions that we hold that are the problem, but rather our level of attachment to those thoughts. This strong attachment, where thoughts are perceived as factual and true, is known as "fusion". Interestingly, fusion is not just a challenge for the thoughts that you may perceive as being *negative* or detrimental to your trading, but also for those that you may perceive as being *positive*. This observation was made by one of my clients when we were working on some strategies to manage thoughts that were not useful in his trading around his current losing run. He stated: *"Actually Steve, if you are having a good run, and you get thoughts of 'I'm having a really good run' or 'I'm really smashing the market at the moment', then they could be equally problematic as they could also cloud your perception and affect your decisions."* He is right. Excessive attachment or fusion to any thought may create a level of interference in your decision processes that is detrimental. Fusion may be one reason behind many traders' lack of ability to reverse their positions in the market, even though this might be the effective action to take. A strong attachment to being long prevents them from shorting. Where traders are able to reduce their levels of fusion, they may also, as a consequence, increase their levels of mental flexibility and extend the range of their trading capabilities.

Jane was a trader who was renowned for her extremely strong views and opinions of the market, despite being a newer trader. I met her for coaching on the recommendation of her desk head who felt that whilst her directional views could sometimes be a real strength for her, within the choppy and volatile markets being experienced at the time, and with an institutional demand for active trading, they might be holding her back. During a couple of meetings we worked together on her ability to be a little less attached – fused – to her thoughts and beliefs, just being able to step back slightly from them using a process known as "cognitive defusion".

- *Cognitive fusion* is the treatment of thoughts as though they are what our minds say they are; thoughts seem like an absolute truth, a command/rule to obey, a threat to get rid of, something happening now even though it's about the past/future, very important.

• *Defusion* recognises thoughts as may/may not be true, they are not a command or rule you have to follow, they may or may not be important, they can be allowed to come and go.

Cognitive Defusion – Changing Your Relationship With Your Thoughts

The difference between being fused to a thought and defused is quite significant. In coaching and workshops I help my clients to understand this psychological process by getting them to write – as big as they can on A4 paper – a key thought or belief that they have identified which inhibits their decision making and performance. I then ask them to hold the piece of paper up, right in front of their nose and ask them what their experience is like, what they can see, where their focus is and what might happen if this thought was held like this in a fused state. Typical responses are that the thought was dominant in their mind, it blocked other thoughts, it was the only thing they could focus on. I then ask them to slowly move the paper away from their nose until they are holding it at arm's length, and again I ask them to notice their experience of this. Now the typical responses include that it was not so oppressive, there was some breathing space, it was possible to see around the thought, it did not feel like you had to act on the thought, it was more relaxed.

Practice: Experiencing Cognitive Fusion and Defusion

• Select a thought or perception that has a "negative" impact on your trading performance.
• Write it down on a piece of A4 paper.
• Bring the piece of paper close to your face so it is in front of your nose. Take a moment to notice what your experience of this is like.
• Now move your piece of paper so it is at arm's length away from you. Take a moment to notice what this experience is like for you.
• Compare the two experiences. What was the same? What was different?

Being aware of the level of fusion you have to a thought or idea can be very useful and a quick and simple way of doing that is to rate it on a 1-to-10 scale or to think about the thought being written on the palm of your hand and to get a sense of how close or far away that thought is from your face – where being closer is more fused and being further away is more defused.

Case Study: Cognitive Defusion in Action

"These markets are impossible to trade right now" was the statement a trader made to me following a difficult start to the trading year.

In my past work I would immediately have been drawn to the use of cognitive behavioural coaching strategies to help the trader challenge that belief and perhaps reframe it (see it differently), or develop a new, more useful belief. However, on this occasion, as I often do now – especially where I sense that the belief is deeply held and/or the train of thinking is not entirely inappropriate for the situation – I started with cognitive defusion.

Here is a summary of how I worked with the trader through a coaching session.

- First I asked him how that thought/belief was affecting him – how did he feel, how was his trading behaviour, what was his experience like?
- Next I asked him whether the way in which he was thinking, and the results he was getting from it – in the context of what he was trying to achieve – was useful. Did it have utility?
- Having established that his current perception was not useful, I taught him some defusion strategies, helping him to change how he related to the thought rather than trying to get rid of or change the content of the thought.

Steve: "How strong is that thought? Show me by bringing your hand towards your face to increase the strength and away from your face to decrease it."

(continued)

The thought, the hand, was virtually on the end of his nose.

Steve: "OK, let's write that thought down on a piece of paper – BIG. Now hold the paper up to the end of your nose. What is that like? What can you see?"

Trader: "Not a lot. Just that thought."

Steve: "And how does that feel? What might your experience be when the thought is right there?"

Trader: "It feels really intense, like I can't escape it and have no choice. I guess I have to do what the thought says."

Steve: "OK, let's try something. Let's put 'I am thinking...' in front of your thought. After all, it is just a thought, right?"

Trader: "I am thinking that these markets are impossible to trade right now."

Steve: "What is that like when you say it? Where would that be in terms of distance?"

The trader moves the paper away from his nose.

Trader: "It feels better. Not quite so in my face – obviously! No, it just gives the feeling of a little more space."

Steve: "Now let's try this, "I am noticing that I am thinking..."

Trader: "I am noticing that I am thinking that these markets are impossible to trade right now."

Steve: "How was that?"

Trader: "Yeah, it feels different. A bit more distant."

Steve: "So where would the paper be now?"

Trader moves the paper even further away from him.

> *Steve:* "OK, so here's an interesting one. Who is doing that thinking?"
>
> *Trader:* "Me."
>
> *Steve:* "No, not you. Your mind... Let's try 'I am noticing that my mind is thinking...'."
>
> *Trader:* "I am noticing that my mind is thinking that these markets are impossible to trade right now."
>
> *Steve:* "What is that like? How is your experience now compared with when we started?"

By this stage the paper is almost at arm's length.

> *Trader:* "It is further away; I feel like I am a bit separated from the thought; it is less intense; I can see more around the room – it is not dominating my focus."
>
> *Steve:* "So the thought is still there, but you feel differently about it? Maybe you could have that thought but without having to act on it. You could have that thought but you could also focus on taking the action you need to take to give yourself the best chance of making good trades, and starting to make money again."
>
> *Trader:* "Yeah, I guess so. It's just a thought, right?"

This is an example of the process of defusion in place. We have not changed the thought, tried to get rid of it or even make it more positive, we have simply altered the way the trader relates to the thought, recognising it as a thought, from the mind, allowing him to assess its utility, giving him some flexibility and space, and importantly allowing him to focus on taking effective action.

Examples of Cognitive Defusion Strategies

Purpose: To see thoughts for what they are not as well as what they say they are.

Method: Expand attention to thinking and experiencing as an ongoing behavioural process.

When to Use: When thoughts/beliefs are functioning as a barrier to achieving desired outcomes.

Strategies
- "I am thinking..." "I am noticing I am thinking..."
- "My mind is thinking..." "I am noticing my mind is thinking..."
- "I don't buy that."
- Observing thoughts mindfully.
- Saying difficult thoughts very, very slowly.
- Is it possible to think that thought as a thought and still carry out the action you have identified?
- Carry cards with difficult thoughts on as a reminder that they are just thoughts.
- Write the thoughts/perceptions down on a piece of paper.

Sit Down, Stand Up – Focus On Effective Action

When I work with traders who are experiencing challenges in their trading they will often be aware of what they want to be doing, but they are not doing what they want – as discussed earlier in this book – and it can often be their thoughts, emotions and feelings that are the barriers to this. By being able to work with your thoughts more effectively, being more open to them and less attached to them, you begin to develop the psychological flexibility that allows you to take effective action more often.

Try this. Sit down somewhere comfortable and safe. In your mind, start to tell yourself to "sit down" repeatedly and with intensity. Repeat the thought over and over again, and then when you have a strong sense of that thought, keep saying it but at the same time stand up.

What was your experience like?

If you are like most people I have conducted this simple experiment with, you will find that despite saying the thought with some intensity and repetition to yourself you were still able to stand up. Maybe it was a little harder, or a little slower, but you did it. The only people who generally stay seated are people who think it is some kind of hypnotic exercise and so even though they could stand up they stay seated to comply with their presupposed response to the situation – which is interesting in itself. This is a key idea based on the proposition that it is possible to hold one thought in your mind and yet be able to take an opposing action. It is possible, for example, to feel extremely tired, to tell yourself *"I can't get up"* and yet actually to get up. Thoughts, emotions and feelings influence your trading behaviour but do not control it. You can hold the thought *"I'm worried about losing money, I need to get out of this trade"* whilst also being able to stay in the trade, provided you have a sufficient level of awareness and also a strong commitment to taking the effective action in that situation.

Reappraisal – Mental Flexibility

The real voyage of discovery consists not in seeking out new landscapes but in having new eyes.
                              Attributed to Michael Proust (1871–1922)

A further process that you can utilise to help you manage your trading experiences is reappraisal. "Reappraisal" is the term used by neuroscientists for *looking at an event differently* – that is, making a new appraisal of it – and is what psychologists call *"reframing"*. It is the way in which stressful events can be reconstrued as beneficial, meaningful or useful. One study[3] showed that mindfulness practice leads to increased *"positive reappraisal"* and reduces feelings of stress. The lens through which we see an event affects how we feel about the event and how we respond to it; developing mindfulness helps to shift that lens.

Having the mental flexibility to look at events with *"new eyes"* is a skill that can be practised and developed. A very simple way of starting to look at challenging events differently can be to ask:

> "How am I seeing this situation? How am I thinking and feeling about it?"
> "Is this useful in terms of what I am trying to achieve?"
> If not, "How else could I see this situation in a way that might be more useful?"

Of course we are back to utility here. Some useful perspective, appraisal questions are:

> "What could I learn from this experience?"
> "How could this experience make me a better trader?"
> "What is the opportunity here?"

These questions are developmental, and suggest a positive benefit from the situation being experienced. They are the ones I used with a young trader who, after about 18 months of trading, was undergoing a period of drawdown. He was finding the whole experience very stressful and was obsessed with focusing on the money he was losing during this period, the impact it was having on his own results for the year and his performance relative to his peers. When it came to utility, he stated that this was obviously not a useful way of thinking about his situation and so we explored some other alternatives. This is a key part of the reappraisal process, examining other options, as you may not hit upon the most effective one first time. I asked him the question: *"What do you think you could learn or benefit from during this time, and as a young trader how could this help your development?"* A shift in mood occurred, and an engaged discussion followed. The trigger had been the word *development*. By being able to see this

period as developmental, as an *opportunity* to gain something –
skills, knowledge, experience – that would be part of becoming
a better trader, he was able to experience a different response.
From a brain perspective, viewing something as an opportunity
rather than a threat has a significant impact on your emotional
response. A threat triggers your avoidance pathways, closing
down creativity, risk taking and experimentation, which is not
ideal when these are exactly the qualities you need at a time
like this. Being able to see something as more of an opportunity
engages the approach mechanisms of the brain, allowing you to
be more flexible, engage with greater energy and be more creative in your actions.

Memories – Thoughts from the Past

On a visit to Asia I was asked by a fund manager: *"How can I
get rid of the memory of the big loss I took earlier this year?"* This
is an interesting question. Memories from the past can, for
some traders, become interference that affects their trading
decisions.

Take a moment to reflect on your own experience of any memories you have that may interfere with your own trading.

One trader I coached had a long-standing *fear* – memory – of
non-farms payroll data, despite being an excellent trader over
data releases. On discussing this and working it through with
him, he revealed how several years ago he had lost a lot of
money on non-farm payrolls and this loss had put him off trading it again. His brain had made a simple connection between
losing a large amount of money and the event, non-farm
payrolls. This is indicative of the generalised way in which
memory works. With further questioning it came to light that
he had not been very well prepared for the data, had taken
quite a big position in the market and when the market had
moved against him, he had not got out where he should have
done and the result of this was a big financial (and emotional)
loss. When I worked this through with him I helped him to

understand that it was not non-farm payrolls that had caused the big loss, but rather as a younger, less experienced and skilled trader his lack of preparation, excessive position taking and unwillingness to take a loss had been the behaviours that led to the loss. His context now in terms of experience, skill and risk management was very different, as expressed when trading other data; breaking the link between the loss and non-farms was key to helping him move forward. However, because of the generalised nature of memory and the emotions attached to the event, we discussed that thoughts and memories of the past may still arise and that by being able to recognise these as a memory from the past – at brain level, recurring as a self-protective mechanism (albeit with very non-specific data) – and being able to observe this process without getting *stuck in it*, along with a commitment to action, he was able to resume his trading of the payrolls data.

This generalised way of thinking about the past also happens when traders reflect on periods of trading when perhaps the P&L was low/negative and the period itself would be described as *bad*, even though there may have been days or even weeks when positive P&L or progress was made. Being specific about a memory is not easy, as Mark Williams – a leading researcher in mindfulness – and his team at Oxford University discovered.[4] They found that if you have experienced a traumatic memory in the past, such as a big loss or a losing run, or if you are exhausted, depressed or locked into a *negative* thought cycle then memory often switches from being specific – which tends to occur if, for example, you recall a time when you felt happy – to more general, retrieving a summary of events (what is known by psychologists as an *"over-general memory"*). People who think in this way tend to have trouble letting go of the past and are more affected by things going wrong in their lives right now and rebuilding their lives after an upset. An interesting study[5] by Richard Bryant working in Sydney, Australia found that firefighters who showed this over-general memory pattern when they joined the fire service were later found to suffer greater trauma from witnessing stressful parts of their job. Another study found that people with an over-general memory were more likely to suffer post-traumatic stress disorder after an assault.[6] This memory tendency is also associated with brooding and with feelings of permanence and irreversibility. The feeling that things are irreversible, or that you have been damaged forever, is very toxic. This is also enhanced by a tendency to suppress memories of events we don't like or by brooding on them – suppression and brooding are both exhausting. Once we get to general we don't tend to return to specific. The research by Williams and his team showed that 8 weeks of mindfulness training makes memory more specific and less over-general, reducing the impact of past difficult or traumatic experiences. This will help traders such as my client in Asia to deal with losses or losing runs, for example, more effectively, not by getting rid of the memory, but rather by changing *how* they remember the events and their impact going forward.

When to Follow Your Mind

The mind does a lot of thinking; you hold views, opinions and beliefs and you create perceptions. Most of this occurs unconsciously, some of it you may have some conscious awareness of. The mind wanders; it can be useful and have utility, or not. The big question is: *"How do you know when to follow your mind?"* Steven Hayes, founder of and leader in the field of acceptance and commitment therapy,[7] suggests that this will be a combination of judgement and experience. Both of these are developed over time, and as your awareness grows you may also notice that your experience broadens and your judgement improves.

Ultimately, however, the key to following thoughts or not comes down to utility:

"Is this thought, belief or perception moving me in the direction I want to go?"
"Is this thought helping me, or getting in my way?"

Three Steps to Managing Thinking

In summary, here is a three-step process to manage your mind's thoughts and cognitions more effectively.

1 *Awareness*

Practise mindfulness to develop a greater awareness of your thinking and cognitions. From an observer perspective, notice your thoughts as thoughts – as mental events; relate and attach to them differently.

2 *Acceptance*

Open up and work with your thoughts. Move away from suppression and towards an acceptance of your thoughts in that moment.

3 *Action*

Keep a key focus on effective action, remembering that thoughts can influence your behaviour but that they do not control the behaviour and actions that you take.

5

Embracing Emotions

Emotions and Trading: A New Paradigm

In 2006 I had a very interesting meeting with a professor of finance in London, at a university where they were launching a new Master's degree in Financial Trading. We had a good discussion about the world of trading and he was very much a believer that the future of trading was automation – he saw a terminator-style rise of the machines occurring over the next few years. He told me that as a result of this trend in trading, the university's Master's programme was based entirely around automated trading and as an aside he also suggested that I might possibly like to consider a new career as, within the next few years, there would be very few human traders left for me to work with. His perspective was certainly indicative of the trend at the time – the rise of the machines – however, during the financial crisis of 2008, many banks turned off their automated trading systems (some of which had lost huge sums of money) and encouraged the "humans" to take over the reins. The human ability to adapt to changing and unfamiliar situations, to sense the markets, apply experience and make judgement calls in conditions of uncertainty was their advantage. Sensing and feeling the markets and making judgements are affective (feeling) skills, and ones which computers do not yet possess – although "affective programming", giving trading black boxes emotions and feelings, is currently in development. So, interestingly, whilst many human traders talk of trading without emotion, at the cutting edge of computer programming are efforts to enable computers to trade with emotion.

I work with a lot of traders in one-to-one coaching and workshops, and one repeated request that I encounter is: *"Can you help me to trade without emotion – I have a great trading strategy and I know that without emotions getting in my way I could significantly increase my returns."* In a recent online seminar I held, 79% of attendees indicated that they would like to be able to trade without emotion. Is this the same for you? Would you also like to be able to trade without emotion?

The reality is that you could not trade without emotion, and when you understand this and the role that emotions play in your decision making you would not want to. As Professor Sam Wang, a neuroscientist at Princeton University, states: *"Emotions are organised brain responses to events in the world around us. So basically emotions are ways to organise or ways of dealing with information. Emotions keep our brains focused on critical information and motivate us to shape our behaviour to gain what we desire and avoid what we fear. In most cases you only have your intuition to go on. You need an emotional factor in decision making to appreciate possible outcomes of a decision. Most real life decisions cannot be based entirely on logic as the information that we have is usually incomplete or ambiguous."*[1] That is a challenging statement for many traders, who have spent years in the quest for trading with zero emotion to absorb; yet it is sound, and based on neuroscientific research. It follows on from earlier work done by Antonio Damasio, author of *Descartes' Error*,[2] who conducted extensive research into the role of emotions and decision making and concluded that emotion and affect are integral to all decisions, that cognition and emotion are intertwined in the decision-making process, beautifully referred to as *"a dance between affect and reason"* by Paul Slovic.[3] Interestingly, as you can see in Figure 5.1, when you look at how the brain processes information, not only is emotion a key part of the decision process, it is the first part of it. You are

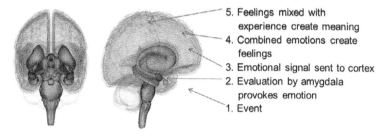

5. Feelings mixed with experience create meaning
4. Combined emotions create feelings
3. Emotional signal sent to cortex
2. Evaluation by amygdala provokes emotion
1. Event

Figure 5.1 The information-processing pathway in the brain.

feeling before you are thinking. Emotions help you to decipher whether something is a risk to be managed or an opportunity to be taken advantage of. Knowledge communicated via emotions, either explicitly or implicitly, enables traders to make fast and efficient decisions and contributes to situational awareness.

If emotion is inextricably linked to your decision process, and in fact a key component of it, then your goal in trading should not be to trade without emotion, as that – even if it were possible – would actually compromise the effectiveness of your decisions. Rather, I would suggest that the goal is to work with your emotions, to be more in tune with them, to improve your ability to coordinate and refine your thinking and feeling processes to enhance your decision making.

Some research has gone as far as to conclude that the people who actually have the most intense feelings, and are able to distinguish between them most effectively, have higher decision-making performance; the key differentiator in decision making may not be the actual emotions or feelings themselves, but how people experience them and what they do with them as they arise.[4] Helping traders to experience, open up to, work with and embrace their emotions is a different approach from what many traders will be using, and is the essence of the mindfulness-based approach presented in this chapter.

Emotions can, of course, affect our decisions, shaping our perception and behaviour, especially where these emotions are towards the extreme – intense anger, panic, great overconfidence, etc. So whilst in *TraderMind* the underlying principle is to work with, to embrace, emotions, this sits alongside the processes of regulating emotion and also taking effective action – of which a key aim is to minimise the amount of psychological interference we expose ourselves to in the first place.

The focus on effective action is paramount in the *TraderMind* framework, and sometimes this action will have to be taken in the midst of emotions that may not be conducive to it. For example, there may be a feeling of fear on entering the market, perhaps emanating from a series of previous losses. However, if there is a good trading opportunity then the effective action would be to take the trade, even though you have the feeling of fear. The feeling of an emotion and the taking of an action are separate events and it is possible to feel a feeling and act differently, as we examined with thoughts in Chapter 4. You can feel tired and yet get out of bed. You can feel hungry and yet not eat anything. You can have a sense of fear and yet still enter the market; or a feeling of anxiety when in the market and still stay in a trade. Emotions bring an urge for action but we do not have to take that action. It is possible, with practice and through awareness and commitment, to feel an emotion, even to embrace it and explore it, and yet not have to act upon it. All of this becomes easier with practice and particularly through mindfulness training.

So where do we stand with the role of emotion in trading? Dr Kevin Oschner, director of Columbia University's Social Cognitive Neuroscience Laboratory in the USA, has this to say: "*While I agree in general with the benefits of regulating emotion there is the important caveat that cognition and emotion are not enemies of one another. You need to have your thoughts guided and informed by emotional responses. There are certain kinds of judgements we make that are necessarily emotional. The goal is not to be an emotional ice cube that is dispassionate and computer like. The goal is not to let emotions overwhelm you to such an extent that you have no cognitive resources leftover.*"[5]

From the neuroscience research, three key guiding principles emerge that I believe are important for traders to understand and act upon if they are to enhance their decision making and performance:

1 Emotions are essential to the decision process.
2 Emotions are data – they provide messages about your experience and give feedback that contributes to your situational awarenss.
3 Emotions cannot be controlled – but they can be regulated/managed.

These three key principles are a significant shift away from many traders' beliefs, but being open to them, and embracing them, are key if you are to manage your emotions effectively in trading. They are also very well aligned with a mindfulness-based psychological approach, which encourages you to be open to and accepting of your emotions, whilst also providing strategies and techniques that enable you to manage them and regulate them effectively.

Emotional Awareness

The first step towards being able to work with your emotions and manage them more effectively is to develop a greater awareness of them, to start to notice them. This is a point highlighted in research conducted by Mark Fenton-O'Creevy and his team from the Open University, who suggest that the focus on emotions in trading should be the development of greater self-awareness of emotional states not their elimination.[6] According to Travis Bradberry, only 36% of people studied in his research on self-awareness were able to accurately identify their emotions as they happened – having good emotional awareness. For the other two-thirds of people this lack of emotional awareness – being less skilled at recognising their emotions in real time – means that they are far more likely to be driven and controlled by their emotions.[7] How about you? How is your emotional awareness? A simple first step towards developing your emotional awareness could be to start "checking in" at times throughout the day.

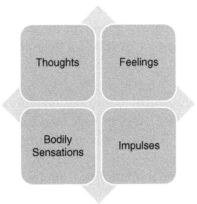

Figure 5.2 What makes an emotion?

Mark Williams looks at emotions as having four components, as shown in Figure 5.2.[8] There is an interplay between thoughts, feelings, impulses and bodily sensations that he suggests creates our emotional experience. One way of developing your emotional awareness is to periodically stop and start to notice, pay attention to the elements of your emotional experience, ask yourself:

- What thoughts am I noticing?
- What feelings are present?
- What impulses am I aware of?
- What bodily sensations do I have?

You could also develop your awareness based upon the emotions as data idea in a very simple three-step process:

1 What am I feeling right now in this moment?
2 What is the message/data behind the feeling?
3 What effective action should I take?

Another way to develop your emotional awareness could be to keep a running record of whatever emotions you notice throughout the day, to write them down and create a "ticker tape" of emotional data. Alternatively, you can just start to notice your emotions in the moment, naming them as you experience them – a process known as "affect labelling" – and as you will see later in this chapter, a very effective emotional regulation strategy.

If you want to gain a deeper emotional awareness, then the *Mindfulness of Body and Breath* practice below is a great way of doing so. This practice has multiple benefits for traders. Firstly, the mere act of practising it creates the metacognitive awareness and attention capabilities for you to regulate your emotions. Secondly, through the practice you are – as we have discussed previously – developing neurological changes, for example to your amygdala (the emotional radar), that will impact how you process emotions and reduce your emotional reactivity. Thirdly, by paying attention to your breath you are creating a connection to it, and will, over time, be sensitive to changes in it and the emotional states that it reflects. Fourthly, with the focus on the body, alongside your breath, you are developing your "interoceptive" ability, the ability to be aware of your own internal signals. A high level of interoceptive ability has been linked to a person's ability to regulate their emotions – awareness first, regulation second.

Practice: Mindfulness of Body and Breath

- Start by sitting comfortably in an upright position or by lying on a comfortable surface.
- Bring your attention to the physical sensations of the body, starting by bringing an awareness to the points of contact you have with the floor/chair.
- Now bring the "spotlight of attention" to your feet – the soles, heels, toes and tops of the feet – noticing any sensations that may be present, or the sensation of no sensations, whatever is there. Hold your attention here for a few moments.
- Now repeat this process of shining the spotlight and holding an awareness for a few moments as you move through the body: legs, stomach/lower back, chest/upper back, arms, shoulders, neck, head.

(continued)

- Now bring an awareness to the whole body, paying attention to the body as a whole.
- Next bring your attention to the breath as it moves in and out of your body.
- Allow your attention to move to the physical sensations of breathing in the abdomen/stomach; the rise and fall, the stretch of the skin.
- As with all practices, if you find your mind wandering, simply notice it, acknowledge where your mind had wandered to and then bring it gently back to your point of attention, the part of the body or the breath as appropriate.
- Stay with this practice for 10 minutes, or more as you develop your skills.

Since I have been working on the mindfulness exercises one thing I have noticed is a reduction in my emotional mood swings.

Trader

Developing emotional awareness is the first step towards embracing emotions, it is also a precursor to being able to regulate them – although interestingly awareness alone acts as a regulator, helping you to reduce the impact of more extreme and intense emotions on your trading decisions, reducing the number of bad trades you make and then the subsequent spirals that can occur as you seek to correct them and recover losses.

Developing your own emotional awareness can also help you to get a greater awareness of the emotions, the sentiment, of the market. "*We simply attempt to be fearful when others are greedy, and greedy when others are fearful*" states Warren Buffett. Meanwhile Mark Cook, interviewed in *Stock Market Wizards*,[9] talks about how he uses his own fear to know when the right time to buy is. He figures that if he is feeling scared, then most of the market probably is too. Being in tune with your own emotions can put you in tune with the market, and enable you to get an edge from it.

Embracing Emotions – From Avoidance to Acceptance

Take a moment to complete the exercise below.

> **Reflection**
>
> *What emotions, feelings, impulses, urges or sensations do you fight with, avoid, suppress, try to get rid of or struggle with?*

In my workshops, when I am delivering training on being more open to our trading experiences, our thoughts and emotions, I often do an exercise with the group where I get them to form a circle facing inwards and select two people from within the group without indicating to anyone who they are. I then ask them to assign person 1 to be all the positive experiences they love to feel in trading and person 2 to be those experiences that they do not like. I then ask them, on my command, to stay as close to person 1 as possible whilst at the same time staying as far away from person 2 as possible. The result is a frantic game of race and chase until I call a halt to the proceedings. I then ask them to try and keep person 1 and 2 at an equal distance apart. From the start this second task has a different dynamic – not as frantic, more measured, calmer – and 99% of the time it ends in a stable equilibrium. It is a great physical experience of how we try to cling on to what is deemed good, and avoid what is deemed bad. After a *winning trade* we desire another one, after a *losing trade* we are afraid of having another one. When they have completed the exercise, helping them to understand the importance of noticing their experience – without in that moment trying to change it – whilst focusing on taking effective action becomes much easier. A combination of awareness and acceptance enables you to take the observer position in your experience, creating a gap between stimulus and

Figure 5.3 Observing emotions, accepting vs. avoiding.

response, a space where there is choice and flexibility, and where you can move from reacting to responding (Figure 5.3). In doing so you will be more able to shift away from the clinging and aversion pattern that is so easily established and played out in the rollercoaster world of trading, and you will be able to achieve greater emotional stability and greater clarity of mind.

From a neuroscience perspective, and if you are to embrace the "emotions as data" concept, then all emotion is useful emotion as it provides valuable information and energy to act. In fact, just embracing that concept – that all emotions are useful, and there are no *bad* or *negative* emotions – can immediately reduce your aversion and defensiveness to emotions such as fear, anger, regret and shame. Most of your emotional responses might be entirely appropriate for the situation you are in. Most traders might have a very similar response – this is known as a *"clean"* or *"primary"* emotion. Fear may be warning us of a potential threat in the market, excitement may be alerting us to an opportunity. Traders need to have an awareness of all that they are feeling if they are to train and maximise the benefit from their internal risk/reward barometer. An openness to emotions, including those such as fear, and their risk/reward function is evident in this piece from Ed Seykota:

Risk is a combination of the possibility of a loss and the magnitude of the loss. We register risk in our bodies as feelings of fear. One way to man-

age various forms of risk, including prospective risk, initial risk, open risk and unconscious risk is to make sure your feeling of fear is an ally, fully functioning on your emotional instrument panel. In our medicinal culture, some people attempt to mediate fear, rather than manage risk. In general people with willingness to experience fear and other feelings are better risk managers than those who have fear in knots or fear under the influence of narcotics.

www.seykota.com/tribe[10]

By being open to your emotions you are also able to avoid the self-defence mechanisms that arise to stop you from feeling emotions such as shame, regret and fear; that reveal themselves through trading behaviours such as risk aversion, selling winners early, holding on to losers and chasing losses.

A greater openness to emotion also provides a key process in regulating and shaping your experience through what is known as the "exposure effect". By exposing yourself to whatever is present in your field of awareness in the moment, allowing yourself to experience what you are experiencing and refraining from the desire to change it in any way, you are meeting potentially *unpleasant* experiences and turning towards difficulty rather than away from it. This process, although counterintuitive for many people, results in exposure to such experiences – which in turn conditions your ability to cope with them. Often people notice that in the moment their experience changes as they turn towards what they are noticing, and in the longer run continued exposure to these experiences often results in their reduced activation (extinction) or reduced intensity. This is very similar to exposure therapy – a very effective psychological approach where people are exposed to their fears and, through this exposure, learn to manage the fear more effectively and change their fear response.

One trader I introduced to the concept of being more open to his emotions, and more willing to accept them and work with them, had a significant insight into his current psychological approach. He realised that his attempt to fight back and change or control his so-called *negative emotions* was actually reducing his attentiveness to the trading screen and also, through the course of the day, was actually tiring him out. This is typical of our experience when we struggle with our emotions, rather than being more open and accepting of them, and working with them. Trying to control or suppress emotions is possible, but it can be a bit like holding a beach ball under the water – you can do it, but it takes a real conscious effort, allows little attention to go elsewhere and eventually the emotions are going to surface with gusto. Suppression of emotion takes your prefrontal cortex (the thinking, planning and control centre) "offline" and is very cognitively expensive; it impacts memory and learning, making it hard to make sense of the changing market environment. When your tiredness and emotions eventually surface, it is often a process that precedes behaviour such as revenge trading, or excessive risk taking. It is often not your emotions or even the intensity of your emotions *per se* that leads to your unhelpful trading behaviours, but rather your attempts to try to avoid or control these emotions.

In terms of trading decision making the implications of this shift in approach, from avoidance to acceptance, are supported in findings by Fenton-O'Creevy and his team. They found that there was a strong relationship between a trader's emotional regulation strategy, their trading behaviour and their results, with those who used suppression strategies making significantly worse decisions.[6] With suppression and control strategies, traders find themselves experiencing a greater range of what are known as *"dirty"* or *"secondary"* emotions – emotions which arise as a result of your reaction to your *"clean"* or *"primary"* emotions – and so traders may experience anger about being angry, get anxious about being anxious and have a fear of fear. These secondary responses are often the ones that are most unhelpful, and an acceptance of – and working with – emotions at the primary stage plays a big role in reducing this potential. Interestingly, whilst in trading we talk a lot about fear – fear of loss, fear of missing out, fear of being wrong – I have come to realise over the years that probably the biggest fear in trading is the fear of fear.

Practice: Leaning into Emotions

As you experience emotions, be willing to embrace them, open up to them and lean into them. Think about approaching them rather than avoiding them.

- OBSERVE – bring awareness to the feelings in your body.
- BREATHE – take a few deep breaths.
- ACCEPT – what is there.
- ACT – in accordance with effective action for the situation.

Following the outcome of a trade, whether you have won or lost, the feelings that you have will typically colour your next decision. An awareness of this and how you are feeling, opening up and leaning into it, reduces the chances of you acting on these emotions. A movement towards emotions quietens them down; emotions are messengers – data – if you ignore them they will shout louder and louder until the message is heard. By allowing yourself to see how you feel, you are in a better position to make your next decision.

In *TraderMind* you are encouraged to be open to your emotions, and will practise this – being willing to notice and accept the feelings in the moment, whatever they are. This is in stark contrast to models of emotional control and avoidance. However, if emotions are key to your brain's processing of information, if emotions are data and based on evidence the suppression of emotion is actually counterproductive, cognitively demanding and ultimately ineffective, what is the alternative and would you really want it?

Emotional Regulation – Affect Labelling

A large part of your ability to regulate your emotions through mindfulness training is going to come through the neurological changes in your brain and how they affect your information processing and emotional responses resulting from the sustained mindfulness practices, through having a greater awareness of your emotions and being an observer of them, through approaching rather than avoiding them; being more open to them and through the exposure effect that results from this. All of these processes stand to help you make significant shifts in how you experience emotions in your trading and their impact on your decision making. I would, however, like to share some other methods that you can use in the moment to help you regulate your emotions.

One process that has proven to be very effective for emotional regulation and is very mindfulness focused is *affect labelling*. This is a simple process that requires you to name or label emotions as you become aware of them. Research by neuroscientist Matthew Lieberman at UCLA suggests that the enhanced capacity to find words for emotions as you experience them promotes a more effective recognition of such experiences and allows you to regulate them more adaptively – labelling emotions helps to reduce the activation of your emotional system (the limbic system) by engaging the thinking and control centre in the brain (the prefrontal cortex, specifically the right ventrolateral prefrontal cortex) and decreasing amygdala activity (the emotional radar). For many people the idea of naming or *admitting* how you are feeling would be completely counterintuitive, and Lieberman and his team found that same pattern in their research subjects. However, the results of their research studies are compelling.[11] In one study, research subjects performed better on a test when they spent 10 minutes writing about their anxiety versus those who wrote about unrelated topics.[12] In another study, people with a fear of spiders were more willing to approach a spider if they had previously described their anxiety in detail; in fact, the more descriptive they were the closer they got.[12] People incorrectly predict that labelling emotions will make them feel worse. Actually, putting your feelings into words helps to regulate your emotional experience and puts you in a better place to make trading decisions – 'naming and taming'.

An extension of this process could be to write down your feelings. This could be particularly useful after a big win or loss, or during a winning or losing period. Writing down your thoughts and feelings can help stop you from acting them out. This is a process I have used to great effect with many clients; the act of writing their thoughts and feelings down gets them out, into conscious awareness, helps them to observe and relate to the emotions differently, process them and react less to them.

One client described his use of this technique, which I often call the *Daily Download*, like this:

One aspect that I have taken from the coaching that has made a huge difference for me has been taking the time at the end of the trading day to do the Daily Download. Being able to get my thoughts and feelings out at the end of each day has been really helpful. I feel better when I have finished the process, cleansed in a way, and seeing what I have written has given me some useful insights. It reminds me of the Harry Potter films with the Pensieve, when they use the wand to extract their thoughts from their head and then put them into the bowl where they can see them, and observe them. At first it was difficult making myself do this every day, but now, having done it for so long and seeing the benefits, I am more worried about not doing it. It is a bit like flossing – you have to get into the habit of doing it, then you don't want to stop. Flossing is good dental hygiene. The Daily Download is good mental hygiene.

Having never read the Harry Potter books, some quick research on the Internet led me to this:

Dumbledore: *"I use the Pensieve. One simply siphons the excess thoughts from one's mind, pours them into the basin, and examines them at one's leisure. It becomes easier to spot patterns and links, you understand, when they are in this form."*

Something else which is of interest in our mental experience of our emotions can be seen in how we explain our relationship to our emotions. In the Western world, for example, it is common to hear phrases such as *"I am angry"* or *"I am anxious"*. In contrast, in Asia, for example, it is more common to hear phrases such as *"I have anger"* or *"I have anxiety"*. This subtle difference from *"I am..."* to *"I have..."* suggests a different relationship with the emotion; something that is here now, but transient – as is the fleeting nature of emotion – and without the strong sense of attachment and subsequent intensity. A shift in your own language away from *"I am..."* to *"I have..."* – or, as I often suggest, phrases such as *"I am noticing the emotions of...."* or *"I am noticing an emotion I call..."* – as you bring awareness to your emotions can be very useful indeed.

Be aware of your own emotional language; if it could be useful, try something different.

Emotional Regulation – Reappraisal

Another way to regulate your emotional experience is through the use of reappraisal, through changing how you perceive and think about an event, as discussed in Chapter 4. Mindfulness training, as we have seen, in itself increases your *positive appraisal* of events and reduces feelings of stress. When traders are experiencing a challenge within their trading, recovering from a big loss, navigating a period of drawdown, dealing with market change or institutional demands, I will often ask them how they are feeling about events, and then how they are seeing those events. I want them to become aware of the link between their perception and their emotions (Figure 5.4).

Whether we see something as a *threat* or an *opportunity*, for example, can have a significant impact on our emotional experience and subsequent behaviour. A great example of this was a trader – we shall call him James – who was brought into an investment bank with a mandate to build a lower-tier franchise into a top-tier one over a period of years, a task he had

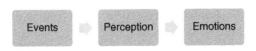

Figure 5.4 Emotions are an outcome of our perception of events.

previously accomplished at a competitor. One of the challenges he faced was that the franchise he was building was undergoing significant regulation and the impact of this was a need for lots of change, including restructuring the desk and trading approaches and strategies. On his arrival at the bank and into his new team, one of his first observations was how much the traders on the desk were focused on the forthcoming regulatory changes and how they were *negative* about this and experiencing feelings of frustration and stress around the changes being made. They were seeing regulation as a threat. James, in contrast, had a completely different perspective on matters. He saw regulation as a period of change and adaptation, which would be financially costly and impact short-term returns, but ultimately as a mechanism which would force lower-tier competitors out of the market due to a lack of ability to finance the required changes to stay competitive, and this would then increase the opportunity in the market for himself and his team. He was seeing events as an opportunity.

Having the mental agility to look at events with *new eyes* is a skill that can be practised and developed. A very simple way of starting to look at challenging events differently can be to ask the three key questions I introduced in Chapter 4:

"How am I seeing this situation? How am I thinking and feeling about it?"

"Is this useful in terms of what I am trying to achieve?"

If not, "How else could I see this situation in a way that might be more useful?"

Emotional Regulation – The Mindful Moment

In the fast-paced world of markets it is not always possible for traders to utilise cognitive strategies for emotional regulation in real time. This is part of the rationale behind engaging in regular mindfulness training to develop your awareness and attention, and create the required neurological changes *offline* to enable you to have enhanced performance *online*. Think about going to the gym as a way of developing the physical fitness required to undertake a job that requires heavy lifting. Mindfulness training is a way of going to the mental gym to develop the mind fitness required to undertake the mental and emotional demands of trading and investing. However, there is also one really quick and simple effective technique that can be used in real time to help with emotional regulation; it is called the *"mindful moment"*.

The mindful moment simply requires you to bring full attention to your breath in the moment, as with the mindfulness of breathing practice. There are many parts to the breath to focus on and I often advise clients to choose a specific part – for example, the rise and fall of the abdomen or chest; the speed or rhythm of the breathing – something that is prominent for them. In the moment, bringing full attention to the breath helps you to get in touch with the feelings that are present at that time, and brings you into the present. If you are experiencing emotions that you want to regulate, it is likely they are at the fear or overconfidence end of the emotional spectrum and towards an extreme in terms of intensity. With such emotional states, thoughts are often arriving from the past, or your mind is diving into the future, bringing unhelpful feelings and sensations.

Practice: Mindful Moment

First practise offline just contacting the breath and being with it
To get in touch with your breath, take a moment to sit comfortably. Place one hand over your belly and feel it moving as the breath moves in and out. Take some time to notice the movements with your hand and then without your hand as time progresses. There is no need to control the breath or breathe in any particular way. Allow it to flow naturally as it will, noticing as best you can the pattern of physical sensations that come with it. Explore the breath and see where your mind naturally comes to attention – perhaps on the abdomen or chest, or on the speed or pauses between the in breath and the out breath, or on the flow of air around the nostrils. Find a place of focus and then allow your awareness to rest there, using it as an "anchor" for the breath in the future.

Real-time application online
In the moment, bring your attention to a part of the breath that you connect with – to your own unique anchor. Bring full awareness to it for as many moments as you need to.

Embracing Emotions in Practice – Running Profits

Rahul was a trader who came to coaching because he was having problems with running his trades to his profit targets. His analysis was good and he was quite sure that if he could hold on to his trades for longer then he would become more profitable. He currently estimated that he was holding his trades for between 30% and 50% of his intended profit.

Steve: "Go back to a time when you were holding a trade. What is that like?"
"How does it feel?"
"What thoughts are you having?"
"What sensations are there?"
"What actions are you thinking of taking?"
"When you get out of the trade what happens?"
"Later, after you have exited the trade, what is your experience like?"

Rahul: "If the trade doesn't reach my profit level I am happy, well I am not really because I didn't stick to my plan; but all too often the market is going to my full profit level and I feel frustrated that I didn't hold the trade for longer. I am not backing up my analysis. I am letting myself down."

Steve: "OK, so it is interesting to notice that in the short term you feel better when you get out of a trade. The anxiety and worry goes away. Your thoughts change. The tension goes away. That must feel good."

Rahul: "Yes…"

Steve: "But, in the long term, you feel frustration."

So there is a short-term gain, a reduction in the feeling of anxiety and a long-term cost, emotional (frustration) and financial (lost profits). Humans are hardwired for the short term, and the behavioural finance concept of intertemporal discounting, which shows how we value money now more than money in the future, exacerbates this. Combined with a biologically induced focus on short-term thinking driven by the release of stress hormones and the discomfort of the feeling of anxiety, it is easy to see why traders will often seek to reduce short-term discomfort. These forces, acting together, create strong motivation for getting out of the trade. What can I do? How can I get rid of these feelings and stay with my trades for longer?

When you are holding a trade you are in a tricky situation psychologically. If you hold the trade and then it goes against you, you feel really bad that you didn't take the money when you could have; if you take the money then you feel really bad if it hits your profit target. Holding trades requires you to feel uncomfortable – to have challenging thoughts whilst also holding on to the trade. It's a bit like a parachute jump – you are in the plane, the door opens, it is time to jump. Your brain and body are flooded with thoughts, emotions and physical sensations that are probably suggestive of staying in the plane. Yet, with sufficient commitment, people jump; but this is not in the absence of anxiety or fear or worrying thoughts, it is with them.

When we seek to avoid feelings of discomfort, this is known as *"experiential avoidance"*. The key to being able to get through such moments – and this is similar for taking losses, getting into trades and also resisting taking trades – is to be able to manage the short-term discomfort. This means being willing to embrace and stay in contact with the emotions you are feeling and to stay focused on taking skillful and effective action for the situation you are in. It is important to stress here that I am not talking about blindly hanging on to all trades in some kind of mental and emotional endurance test, but rather being able to stay in touch with the emotions that you are feeling with a willingness to open up to some short-term discomfort whilst staying responsive to the market and to your strategy. This may indeed mean at times making judgement calls to get out of a trade early, or take a trade that was not planned, due to the dynamic nature of the markets and the unfolding of events. This will come largely through experience, and through effective reflection on your past trades and rehearsal of future market scenarios.

With a commitment to some mindfulness practice, and a greater awareness of his thoughts and emotions in real time – along with a willingness to embrace and lean into some of the feelings of anxiety that holding a trade brought – Rahul was able to extend his time in onside trades to about 80% of his profit targets.

STOP Struggling and Embrace Your Emotions

The key essence of this chapter, and of the mindfulness-based approach to managing emotions, is of being aware of your emotions, open to them, accepting them in the moment, approaching and embracing them, and in line with the neuroscience findings, seeing them as data, something that is inherently very useful. I fully recognise the giant leap of faith needed by most traders to let go of the struggle to control emotions and move towards embracing them, as it is a shift that I have had to make myself in my own coaching practice. However, the neuroscience studies supporting these approaches are compelling and the real-time utilisation of them by my clients, and the feedback that they have given, only goes further to suggest that it is a leap worth making.

When you talked about how we shouldn't control our emotions but should try and accept them I wasn't so sure. It didn't make sense to me at first. But when I really thought about it I realised that I have been trying to control my emotions in trading for years, and it hasn't really worked. Anyway, I decided to start to notice my feelings and think about what the data might be. It wasn't easy at first, but after a while I have really noticed a difference to how I feel. It's hard to explain but it's like I am more aware of how I feel, but there is less intensity or reaction to them.
Trading client workshop feedback

To finish, here is a great four-step strategy to incorporate the core points of this chapter, and indeed of the book as a whole, into one simple process. This is a great technique to use when you are perhaps in a situation where you can begin to feel your emotions moving towards an extreme.

Slow your breathing, observe, anchor to the present.
Take time to notice – thoughts, feelings, urges.
Open up; breathe into them; make room for them.
Pursue effective action.

6

Managing Urges and Impulses

Urges and Temptations

The ability to think and act quickly and effectively has evolutionary benefits, and obvious benefits to traders in making decisions in the heat of the markets. Making quick, impulsive decisions – such as an unplanned holiday, an evening out or a purchase of some sort – can also be beneficial from a life perspective. However, impulsive actions in the trading environment can also have consequences and a number of trading behaviours that may reduce market returns can be linked to them.

Warren Buffett said that: *"Success in investing doesn't correlate to IQ once you're above the level of 100. Once you have ordinary intelligence, what you need is the temperament to control the urges that get other people into trouble in investing."*[1] What are these urges? Well, they can come in many forms for different traders but common urges that are given when I ask this question of traders in my workshops include the urge to take profit early, the urge to hold on to a loss, the urge to trade when the markets are quiet, the urge not to pull the trigger – perhaps following a previous loss or losing run, the urge to take more risk than usual, the urge to take less risk than usual, the urge to enter the market before being fully prepared and ready for the trading day, the urge to stay at the screen all day long to avoid missing out on an opportunity, the urge to "get back a loss".

Why these urges occur can be explained in a number of different ways, including looking at the research in behavioural finance which highlights a number of trader biases or heuristics (mental shortcuts), or as I prefer to call them *"tendencies"*, that arise out of the uncertainty of the markets. These tendencies are essentially the brain's way of responding to the information-processing demands of making a trading or investment decision and coping with the uncertainty of the environment that it is being made in. The disposition effect leaves traders with a tendency to become risk averse in situations of gain (take profits early) and risk seeking in situations of loss (run losses). Overconfidence might lead to traders taking excessive risk; the *"snake bite effect"* may keep traders out of the market; fear of missing out (FOMO) might keep traders at their screens; and a bias towards action may see traders trading even when they have no edge or strategic reason to do so. One of the key findings from behavioural finance as it relates to traders is that many of a trader's tendencies may be exactly the opposite to those required to be successful as a trader or investor. The evolutionary process has not been focused around adapting to financial markets and becoming successful at trading them.

Of course, there are other processes going on that may contribute to the urges we have. The emotions that a trader is experiencing will also create urges. Feelings of overconfidence or fear will impact on a trader's decision behaviour, as will boredom or excitement. These emotions can be very powerful and often linger outside conscious awareness – unless they are embraced and worked through, as we discussed in Chapter 5. Likewise, as we shall see in Chapter 7, a trader's level of mental and physical fatigue can create tendencies to make decisions in ways that may not be most conducive to maximal market returns. For some traders the urge is noticed most strongly by their own thoughts, which talk them into or out of behaviours that ultimately – in the long term – are not beneficial.

Reflecting On Your Trading Urges

- *What urges do you find yourself experiencing within your own trading?*

- *When do these urges arise?*

- *What action do you take when these urges are present?*

- *What are the consequences of those actions?*

What is an Urge or Impulse?

In the dictionary, an impulse is described as *"a sudden strong and unreflective urge or desire to act"*, whilst an urge is defined as *"a strong desire or impulse"*.

Impulsivity can also be thought of as a tendency to act without forethought, or as having a lack of behavioural inhibition – the ability to stop a behaviour. It could also be seen as acting on the spur of the moment, not focusing on the task at hand or not planning and thinking carefully. Impulsivity can also be a pattern of your behaviour; it can be learnt and becomes a "skill", a repeatable behaviour rather than just a single discrete act.

From a mindfulness-based perspective, many urges, self-defeating or self-destructive behaviours are seen as attempts to escape, avoid or get rid of unwanted thoughts and feelings. This is a very interesting view, especially when we look at it in terms of trading behaviour. For example, if we look at the challenge of taking a trade following a previous loss, or during a losing run, it is common for traders to experience some anxiety about placing a trade, with an urge to *"not pull the trigger"*. The anxiety associated with taking risk in the market, and the feelings of discomfort associated with potential future losses, can be avoided by not taking risk, by not trading, and so in the short term the trader *feels better*. However, by not trading the trader can, of course, not make any money, may see good trading opportunities pass them by and feel they have missed out, and will inevitably in the longer term feel worse. Learning how to manage such urges is important in becoming the best trader you can possibly be, and in achieving the best possible returns from the market.

Mindfulness Training and Urge Reduction

One of the findings of the *Mindfulness Report* was, as we saw in Chapter 1, that people who are more mindful feel more in control of their behaviour and are more able to override and change internal thoughts and feelings and resist acting on impulse. This ability to *override* thoughts and feelings and to *resist* impulses is dependent on having a well-trained "observer" (your impartial spectator), the mental ability to be aware of your experience and to be able to notice any urges and *veto* or *inhibit* them – as discussed earlier in the book when we looked at training attention and awareness and its benefits. Mindfulness training develops this ability and strengthens the neural circuits and brain regions that are responsible for this function.

Urges can be seen as quick actions taken with little conscious awareness, or as an emotional reactivity to a situation or stimulus. By its very nature, mindfulness is quite the opposite.

Let's revisit Jon Kabat-Zinn's definition: *"Paying attention in a particular way: on purpose, in the present moment, and non-judgmentally."* The training and cultivation of mindfulness precludes impulsivity through a maintenance of attention in the present moment and with the qualities of acceptance, openness and curiosity. The more time you spend developing your mindfulness practice the less you may develop some of your urges, the less intense they may become and the greater your ability to manage them will be.

Impulsive behaviour can also be a function of a low emotional regulation capacity and so mindfulness training can help to reduce impulsivity by the increased ability to regulate emotions and in particular by embracing emotions rather than supressing them. In behavioural finance studies it is suggested that biases and shortcuts, traders' tendencies, are pronounced when levels of stress are increased. Mindfulness training increases your resilience, your stress capacity and lowers your stress reactivity, in turn reducing the possible impact of these tendencies or urges on your trading and investing decisions.

Practice: Mindfulness of Urges

Mindfulness exercises can help you notice your thoughts and feelings BEFORE you start the urge behaviour:

Take some deep breaths, notice thoughts and feelings, see if you can identify the ones you are trying to push away from.

DURING the urge behaviour:

Mindfully observe the way you do the problematic behaviour, noticing every aspect in great detail, and in particular notice what thoughts and feelings are present. Often simply bringing full attention to a behaviour disrupts it.

The Changing Nature and Impermanence of Urges

Take some time to complete the practice below.

Practice: Experiencing the Changing Nature and Impermanence of Urges

- Take a seat, with your back unsupported, on a chair or a cushion.
- Bring attention to your breath, as in the mindfulness of breathing practice, whilst also noticing when the mind wanders and, as before, noticing where it has wandered to, acknowledging it and bringing your attention back to the breath.
- Wait for a sense of discomfort to appear – it could be a physical discomfort from sitting in your current position, an itch or a restlessness.
- Notice the desire to move and "get rid of it", and resist it.
- Notice the thoughts that arise: "I wish I could get comfortable", "I wish this itch would go away", "I would love to scratch right now".
- These thoughts are just thoughts, mental events; allow them to be, and bring your attention back to your breath and bodily sensations.
- Notice how discomfort feels, how the feeling of discomfort changes over time, notice how its intensity changes with the breath in and out. Is it stronger on the in breath or the out breath?
- You might find your mind wandering to other matters – the markets, hobbies, partners, things to do. These are still thoughts; gently bring your attention back to your breath and body again.

Source: Adapted from http://www.mindfulness.org.au/urge-surfing-relapse-prevention/.

In this practice, what you have witnessed is the changing nature and impermanence of urges. Urges come and go, the intensity varies, the accompanying thoughts arise, stay and go. By being able to notice the physical sensations of the urge you are turning towards the urge rather than acting on it, directly facing it rather than feeding and reinforcing it. Just like with emotions, there is an exposure effect that occurs when you *stay with* the urge. Over time, by exposing yourself to the urge you create a different response to it, reducing the intensity of the urge and your likelihood of acting upon it. In contrast, every urge acted upon reinforces and strengthens the urge and your potential for acting upon it again in the future, just as suppression of thoughts and emotions ultimately increases them.

Reflecting on Urges

Ask yourself whether there have been times when you did not give in to an urge when it presented itself. Did the urge pass?

Most of us will have had past experiences of urges passing. This is an important strategy to identify, as it can greatly improve self-efficacy (your belief in your ability) to ride out urges. The main message is that urges do not have to be acted upon.

Insights from Addiction Therapy

One group of people who are faced with the challenge of managing urges are addicts – although they would refer to these urges more usually as cravings. G. Alan Marlatt, in his book entitled "Relapse prevention: Maintenance strategies in the treatment of addictive behaviours",[2] likened urges to waves. He noted that urges for any substance use rarely last for very long and that, like waves, they often start out with a low intensity (ripples out in the ocean), building in power (as the wave forms and crests) and then depowering (as the wave breaks). Helping addicts to *resist* their cravings requires them to be able to *ride* the waves of their cravings. Every time an urge is ridden, subsequent urges are potentially weaker in nature and, over time, through exposure to the urges and approaching them, riding them, the intensity and frequency of the urges can be modified and the ability to be less reactive to them increased.

In trading, being able to manage your urges may require you to ride your waves too, in what is known as *"urge surfing"*.

Urge Surfing

The urges and temptations that you experience in trading are likely to be a combination of the inherent uncertainty that trading brings, having to take risk and cope with the outcomes of those decisions, the way that your brain has evolved, your own predispositions, environment and experience. Whilst it is possible to state *"common trading urges"* as at the start of this chapter, the nature of them – their frequency, intensity and underpinnings – will be unique to the individual trader. One thing that is interesting is that as far back as Adam Smith, through to the writings of Jess Livermore and right up to the latest research in behavioural finance and neuroeconomics, these urges have been present. It would appear that, as Jon Kabat-Zinn (leading mindfulness researcher and practitioner) states: *"You can't stop the waves, but you can learn to surf."*

One trader I coached, who was particularly urge driven, had a challenge with staying out of the market and was very prone to overtrading – which was very costly to him in terms of trading costs and whilst he was a capable trader and produced a good annual return, he really felt that if he could be even slightly more selective with his trading then he would be even more profitable, but also would feel that he was a *better trader* as a result. In discussions with the trader it was clear that he enjoyed being active in the markets, he did not like sitting at his desk and not trading, and that through his experience he had developed a pattern of significant overtrading – he was a skilful overtrader. In the short term he felt engaged with the market – actually what he was doing was avoiding the uncomfortable feelings of boredom – even though in the long term it was reducing his market returns. This is a great example of where learning to *surf* can be a very effective strategy.

Urge surfing is a mental training technique that you can use to manage your trading urges and comes from the work of Marlatt. The overall intention of urge surfing is to be able to ride the wave of your urge – the urge to trade to relieve boredom in our example – such that you do not act upon it, knowing that each time you are successful in this you are developing your ability to do so again in the future as the urge intensity decreases through exposure.

Core to urge surfing is using your ability to simply notice your experience of the urge with a sense of openness and acceptance. What sensations are present? What thoughts arise? What emotions are with you? What urge for action do you have? Applying the non-judgemental aspect of mindfulness requires you to do this without evaluating them as good or bad in any way but simply to notice them, objectively for what they are, and in that moment to accept them as best you can for what they are... urges. Often simply acknowledging urges as *urges* – *"here is an urge to trade to recover my loss"*, for example – makes it easier to manage. Verbalising your urges can work like affect labelling for regulating emotions.

One of the many insights that mindfulness teaches us is that our present moment experience is always shifting – impermanence. Thoughts arise and move into and out of your mind, sensations come and go, emotions arise and pass on like the weather in a transient way. Urges are no different. They do not last forever, and your experience of them is continually changing. Sometimes urges leave us, and then come back again, just like waves coming and going.

When you are urge surfing you are *surfing the wave* of your urge. As soon as you start to notice an urge, you are on the wave. Allow yourself to enter a mindful state, observing your experience of the urge, accepting it for what it is (perhaps even noticing it and labelling it as an urge – which in itself can help to depower the sense of urgency to act upon it). As you ride the wave, staying in contact with it, *leaning into it,* you will notice a reduction in the urge's call to action – especially as you ride the urge to the shore. Every time you ride a wave to the shore you have helped future urges to become weaker and you have developed your surfing competence such that it will be easier to surf again.

Of course, some waves are better to surf than others. In some situations, perhaps where you are under stress or pressure from previous losses, or even previous wins, or there is increased uncertainty or volatility within the markets, or where there is a time pressure involved, you may experience these urges more strongly – a bit like becoming a big wave surfer. At these times, in fact at all times, you may find that you only ride the urge for a period of time, and do not achieve the *full success* that you had expected. *Urge surfing,* just like real wave riding, is a skill that is developed through practice and competence will increase through practice, so keep reminding yourself of this. Look forward to opportunities in the markets to practise riding the waves, whether big or small, and keep focused on the progress you are making with your urge surfing. You will soon find yourself able to ride your urges more effectively.

Impulse vs. Intuition

It is important to differentiate at this point that not all bodily signals or thoughts and emotions that we sense, and that create an urge to act, are urges or impulses. Sometimes you receive messages from the body that we would call gut feel or intuitive sensing. Owing to the uncertainty of the market there is a need for traders to be flexible with their decision processes, and so not every deviation from the predetermined plan is necessarily urge driven, and we should recognise our tendency to classify whether it was an urge or an intuition largely in hindsight once the outcome is known. Being able to distinguish between the two is important and will essentially be a function of experience and mindfulness practice, and this is something we will cover in more depth in Chapter 7, where we look at the mind/body connection.

Boredom Trading and the Challenge of Quiet Markets

Simon came to me for coaching, looking for ways to relieve the boredom of trading he had been experiencing during a particularly quiet time in his markets. He was not enjoying the feeling of boredom and wanted to find ways to *"get rid of it"*.

When we met we discussed his experience of *"boredom"* and the thoughts, feelings and urges that came with it. Naturally, the urge to trade, to get involved in the markets, was the strongest of the urges. Managing the experience of *"doing nothing"* was proving very difficult for a trader who thrived on busy and volatile markets.

Take a moment to try this yourself...

Without moving from where you are sitting, just close the book and place it on your lap. You don't need to sit in any particular way, but just gently close your eyes and sit for a minute or two. It's no problem if lots of thoughts pop up, you can let them come and go for now, but see what it feels like to sit and not do anything for just a minute or two.

How was it? Need to do something? Think about something? Have an urge to focus on something?

It is not easy to do *nothing*. The brain is used to stimulation and the trading environment is, of course, a huge potential source of stimulation. Within trading institutions there is an additional pressure on traders to trade during such periods, as the action of sitting and doing nothing is generally not rewarded or encouraged – even when staying out of the markets may be the most effective behaviour from a market returns perspective. *"I can't sit here all day and do nothing"* one trader told me, *"it wouldn't look good with the boss"*. There is in trading a bias towards action.

So what can you do when markets are quiet, and the urge to trade to relieve that boredom (experiential avoidance in action) creeps in?

Firstly, how you manage your experience of boredom is the key psychologically. I would encourage you to approach this experience, to turn towards it and notice the thoughts you are having, the feelings and the sensations within your body. Bring your awareness to the urges to act. By doing so you will move to experiential acceptance, be more able to manage your experience, less likely to act out your *boredom* emotions and thoughts, and more able to focus on taking effective action.

Secondly, boredom itself is not the challenge, it is a feeling that you get; it is what you do behaviourally when you have that feeling that really matters. With my trading client we discussed what action could be taken that would contribute towards his and his desk's performance that could be achieved whilst the markets were quiet. He told me that making a bit more contact with clients and spending time with other traders on the trading floor discussing markets and strategies – particularly some that he did not get to spend much time with – would be useful. Also, taking some time to review his performance year-to-date, getting ahead with some of the administrative tasks that he always left to the last minute and taking some time to recharge, perhaps get to the gym during the trading day, would also be helpful. The challenge, Simon suggested, would be getting motivated to do these actions.

In a state of *boredom*, energy is often low and waiting for the motivation and energy to arrive to enable you to take action may take some time. At times like this action can be the catalyst for motivation and energy, so the key is to identify an action or two and start doing it, and then let the motivation and energy come.

Crucial Moments and Effective Behaviours

All traders have crucial moments, those points in time when the urges and impulses rear their heads, the moment after the loss is realised, the moment after you missed an entry and the move you had anticipated happens, the moment when the price moves towards your stop level, when the markets go quiet, when you are on a winning run. Having an awareness of your own crucial moments is key, and then following this up by identifying the effective behaviour that you will commit to in that crucial moment. Holding an awareness of the times and situations when you are most *"at risk"* and having a clear idea of what action you will commit to in those moments can be extremely useful in helping you to get different and better results. Bringing a mindful awareness to your crucial moments, surfing the urge and keeping a focus on taking effective action is a very effective strategy.

Take some time to list your own personal crucial moments and what would be the effective action to take in those situations.

Crucial Moment	Effective Action

7

Trading With the Body in Mind

Trading Signals From the Body: Physiological Analysis

In a study conducted by neuroscientists Antonio Damasio and Antoine Bechara,[1] participants took part in a computer game known as the *Iowa Gambling Task* where players are presented with four decks of cards. When a player turns over a card they are shown an amount that they have either won or lost. Two of the decks displayed low amounts of money but would, over time, lead to the player making money, whilst the other two decks had higher amounts of money and were therefore more exciting, but would eventually lead to the participant making a loss. The players did not know the make-up of the decks at the start of the game, but over time they managed to figure out which ones to pick from if they wanted to make money in the long run. What Damasio and Bechara noticed in their observations of the study participants is really interesting:

1 The players started to select from the money-making decks before they consciously knew why; what we might call an intuitive, preconscious decision, learnt implicitly (outside of conscious awareness).

2 Whilst playing the game, the players were monitored using biofeedback equipment measuring the electrical conductivity

of their skin. Skin conductivity is one type of what Damasio and Bechara call a *"somatic marker"*, a physiological marker attached to a prior memory, and is highly sensitive to stress, uncertainty and novelty. They observed that a player's skin conductance began to spike when they contemplated taking a card from the losing decks, and this spike steered them away from these *"dangerous"* choices.

The combination of intuition and somatic marker provided a dual process of assimilating what was happening around them; it informed their decision-making process and enabled them to improve their decision making and, over time, move to the more profitable decks. This combination is a sensing and feeling process, an affective process.

Affective Decision Making

Johan Lehrer, in his book *How We Decide*,[2] recounts a decision made by Lieutenant Commander Michael Riley on board the destroyer *HMS Gloucester* in 1991 during the Falklands War. At the end of a long shift on duty in the radar scanning room of the ship, Lieutenant Commander Riley made a vital decision that had potentially very severe consequences. Riley observed a blip on his radar screen moving towards the American battleship *USS Missouri*, and not knowing with any real certainty whether it was an enemy missile or a friendly American plane, he had it shot out of the sky. Four hours later it was confirmed that his instinctive reaction had been right and he had shot down a missile and not an American plane. In a review of his decision, no *rational* (cognitive) basis for his decision could be found and yet he had made the right call. From a game-theory perspective, the odds of two American aircrew being killed measured against the possibility of a battleship being sunk would have justified the decision to shoot – although had it been an American plane brought down, the decision to shoot would have been looked upon very differently post-event and subject to global media scrutiny. What is interesting is that this type of strategic, rational analysis, a cognitive weighing-up process, had not entered Lieutenant Commander Riley's mind.

This incident became a topic of interest to Gary Klein, a neuroscientist with a particular interest in decision making and intuition. After repeatedly analysing the visual data that Riley had been scanning, Klein discovered that the radar blip had not appeared on his screen until 8 seconds after it would have done had it been an American plane, the third sweep of the radar screen versus the first one. This meant that the blip was flying low, at about 1000 feet as opposed to the 3000 feet of a plane. None of these facts were conscious to Riley or *rationally* analysed. His brain and body were telling him something was wrong – that it was a threat – and his training told him to take action and have it shot down. It had been a feelings-based, affective decision.

Feeling the Markets

You are a sensing and feeling being not just a cognitive one, although we are heavily biased in the Western world towards cognition and rational thinking. The topic of gut feel and intuition in trading decisions is a popular one, with people tending to fall into one of two camps – either being very much against it and any notion of it, instead believing in the importance of removing emotion and feelings from decision making to make it more *rational*, or sitting in the opposite camp where feelings are regarded as a key part of the decision process. Tales of traders making decisions based on "feelings" are quite common in the markets, and George Soros is one particular advocate of relying on his emotions: *"As a fund manager, I depended a great deal on my emotions. That was because I was aware of the inadequacy of knowledge."*[3] He cited acute back pain as a signal that something might be wrong in his portfolio – a somatic marker, a physiological indicator.

In what has become an increasingly intellectual and quantitative trading environment, where rationality is prized, intuition and gut feel have, to some degree, been squeezed out and forgotten, a trend echoed in this quote from Einstein: *"The intuitive mind is a sacred gift and the rational mind is a faithful servant. We have created a society that honours the servant and has forgotten the gift."*

When you take in information from the market you are doing so via your senses, so you are literally sensing the market, and as this information comes into your brain it does so (as we saw when we looked at emotions and decisions) through the amygdala, where emotion is attached before information is sent up to a higher part of the brain, the neocortex. Alongside this, the brain is also receiving signals from throughout the body through interoceptive (meaning 'perceiving within') pathways giving data on heart rate, blood pressure, body temperature, muscular tension and so on. The brain and body are part of one integrated system working together to make sense of the world around you, make decisions about it and act upon them (Figure 7.1).

Intuition, your preconscious decision making, is not something magical or mystical but is developed through experience and draws upon past memories to inform future ones. It is pattern recognition. These patterns are often learnt implicitly – through experience rather than direct teaching – outside of conscious awareness. An event stored in memory also comes with bookmarked bodily sensations, somatic markers, such as physical signs like Soros's back pain, or a tightness in the stomach or elevated heart rate that help us decide what to do in similar situations.

Gut feel allows you to rapidly assess whether a pattern or choice will most likely lead to a pleasant or nasty outcome, whether we

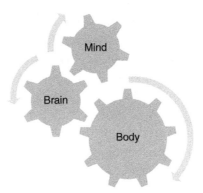

Figure 7.1 *TraderMind* advocates an integrated system of brain, body and mind, an interconnectedness that is required to optimise your trading of the markets.

like or dislike it, welcome or fear it. Gut feel comes from the gut but not just from the gut – information is received from across the body, as described previously via an extensive network of nerves that run throughout your body. Your gut is a part of your enteric nervous system and has 100 million neurons (like the neurons within the brain, and in fact it is called the second brain); it provides data to the brain via a superhighway known as the vagus nerve. Your brain is not just in your head, it runs throughout your body.

Damasio states the importance of these affective processes in making decisions and describes how *"affect gives important physiological cues enabling efficient thinking"*.

Good judgement and decision making in the markets may therefore require the ability to listen carefully to – and get good feedback from – the body, to utilise intuition and somatic markers, to feel as well as to think. This is an ability that some people may have more of than others, and it may provide some insight as to why some traders are able to make great market calls based on their analysis and research but are unable to profit from them.

What Separates Analysts From Traders?

On a coaching assignment to a global energy company I was asked to work with the head economist who had recently started running his own book, trading his own analysis and forecasts, and who was also running a small team of analysts each of which had similarly recently started running their own books. The head economist was perplexed, not just by his own lack of returns based upon his market analysis but more so by the difficulty that his team was having in taking risk based upon their own analysis. He asked me whether I would be able to provide coaching to his analysts to get them to be more confident in taking risk and trading their own ideas. As it was, budget cuts and some restructuring within the organisation meant that I never got engaged in the coaching role, but it is one of those discussions that has always stuck in my mind and that I have given thought to. In fact, I have on a number of occasions been asked about, or engaged to work with, traders who have a great call of the markets and yet are unable to profit from their calls – even if other traders around them are. My initial thinking was that from a personality perspective there are most likely people who are excellent at analysis and can make great market calls, and yet for a number of potential reasons lack the confidence to be wrong, are risk averse in type or do not have the psychological resilience to deal with the highs and lows that trading outcomes inevitably bring. However, on reading Richard Peterson's book *Inside the Investor's Brain*,[4] another insight came to mind, and one which is highly relevant to this chapter.

There is a measure of personality type known as the *Myers–Briggs Type Inventory* developed by Isabel Briggs-Myers and her mother Katharine Cook Briggs based on the work of pioneering psychologist Carl Jung. One of the measures of this test is an axis assessing "Thinking and Feeling", which can be equated crudely and simplistically to rational decision making and emotional decision making.

In Peterson's book he refers to a study conducted by trader coach Doug Hirschorn in the USA which evaluated a large number of portfolio managers and analysts and turned up some very interesting results (Figure 7.2): 80% of portfolio managers

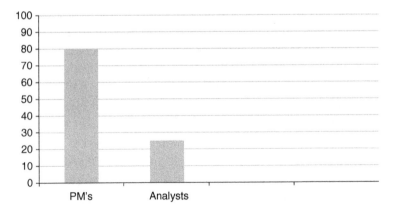

Figure 7.2 Feelings scores resulting from US study of portfolio managers and analysts.

(traders) scored high on feeling, whilst only 25% of analysts did. This finding suggests that one difference between being a good analyst and a good trader may be down to the ability to use feelings (gut feel and intuition) as part of the decision process. As Stanley Druckenmiler says: *"You need a certain amount of intelligence, but it's wasted over a certain level. After that it's more about intuition."*

Can You Really Trust Your Gut?

The *thinking* brain is good for building and understanding models for how the world of trading works, while the *feeling* brain is good at recognising risks and opportunities in the uncertainty of the markets, and making decisions based on them. Paul Slovic, who developed the *Theory of Affect Heuristic*,[5] finds that in simple decision making, conscious thought usually leads to better decisions, but after a certain level of informational complexity is reached, the quality of conscious choice falls below that of affective choice. This is a point shared by Gerd Gigerenzer in his book *Risk Savvy*,[6] which looks at the challenge of making decisions under conditions of uncertainty. He suggests that as uncertainty increases we should aim for simplicity and feel in our decision making, and stick to "rational thought" and complexity when in a risk environment where all the probabilities are known. This indicates that at some point, where there is uncertainty, our intuition and gut feel may be more helpful to us than our *rational* thought. That is a very interesting perspective, and has, of course, real relevance to the trading and investing environment.

The big danger when talking about intuition and gut feel is that they become perceived as something magical and mystical, when in fact – as we touched upon earlier in the chapter – nothing is further from the truth. Intuition and gut feel are the result of experience, something noted by neuroscientist and decision researcher Gary Klein[7] in his work with firefighters, paramedics, fighter pilots and military personnel. One of Klein's key findings was also that experts often had an intuitive feel about a decision first and then evaluated that decision from a cognitive perspective. This is, of course, entirely complicit with how we know information processing in the brain works – feeling first and then thinking. *"Intuition will tell the thinking mind where to look next"* as Jonas Salk, author of *Anatomy of Reality: Merging of Intuition and Reason* and who developed the polio vaccine, states.[8] So it is not simply a matter of blindly following your intuition or your gut, but rather not blindly ignoring them – which may, in fact, potentially lower your market returns. Often your intuition and feel can point you in the direction of a trading or investing idea, pointing you in the direction of potential opportunity, and you can then activate your *thinking* processes to test it further. It can also be a warning light to potential danger. *"If your intuition is flashing danger signs about some course of action or some personal relationship, I urge you not to ignore those signs"* states former "Turtle Trader" Curtis Faith.[9] Decision making is, as Paul Slovic states, *"a dance between affect and reason"* and that affect will incorporate emotion, feelings and physical markers.

One interesting question I often get asked by traders is how do I know if it is intuition or gut feel, or just me wanting something to happen, an urge or impulse. This is not an easy question, and my stock answer to date has been that it is a distinction developed through experience and training. However, in her book *Market Mind Games*, Denise Shull[10] provides an interesting way to differentiate between the two, stating: *"If a feeling feels urgent, if it feels compelling, suspect it as an impulse, if on the other hand it feels calm, if it is a sense coming out of nowhere, consider it as a recognition of something you know but aren't conscious of yet."*

John Coates, neuroscientist and ex-Wall Street trader, suggests that the rise of the high-frequency trading and black-box algorithms has made the market environment a tough one for traders. However, in the ensuing battle between man and machine he identifies a trend in some banks of pulling their black-box systems and putting money back into the human traders, and maybe with very good reason. "*Our ability to generate gut feelings makes our body the most sophisticated black box on the market,*" he states.[11] If you think of yourself in that way then it can be very empowering as a trader, and if you can tap into your black-box potential then you could open up the possibilities of increasing your market returns.

So, how can you develop your intuitive ability and gut feel? How can you form a greater connection between mind and body?

Developing Your Intuition and Gut Feel, Reconnecting the Mind and Body

We can spend too much time in our heads and not enough time in our bodies. Trading by nature involves you in planning, remembering, analysing, judging and comparing processes, and the trend towards quantitative approaches – the left brain and intellect – has driven this further. Over time, such a focus can end up in a disconnection between our minds and bodies, which can not only affect our decision-making process, but also our physical and mental well-being. Mindfulness training can help you begin to fully integrate with your body once again.

Mindfulness practice can help you tune in to your intuition and be more sensitive to your gut feel and bodily sensations, and in so doing help you make more effective trading decisions. Practising mindfulness helps to strengthen these abilities through its focus on your moment-to-moment physical sensations. Through mindfulness, you become more sensitive to and in touch with the sensations that your body is sending; you become able to notice these intuitive and physical feelings earlier and integrate them more effectively into your decision-making process. You develop your interoceptive capacity – your ability to perceive your own internal state – which assists with the perception of emotional and feelings-based events. There are other very effective methodologies for developing interoception, including the use of biofeedback software, which can help traders to become more attuned to their physiology, both in training off the desk and in terms of assessing it while on the desk. The beauty of mindfulness training is that it is easy to learn, practical and take-anywhere, and technology and cost free.

To develop your ability to become more in tune with your body, to be able to notice the subtle shifts in sensations, to develop your interoception and intuition, I would highly recommend the following *Body Scan* practice.

Practice: Body Scan

- Lie down on your back, making yourself comfortable. Close your eyes if you feel comfortable doing so. (*Note:* Some people may prefer, or find it more comfortable, doing the practice sitting down – that is perfectly OK).
- Take a few moments to bring your attention to the physical sensations in your body, noticing the points of contact between your body and whatever you are lying on.
- Remind yourself of the intention behind the practice, to develop an awareness of your experience, without any need to change it. To notice all the sensations within your body as you scan through it.
- Start by bringing an awareness to your breath, and to the sensations in your abdomen. Become aware of the changing patterns in your breathing.
- Imagine a spotlight of attention, and bring this to your feet and toes, noticing any sensations present there and investigating them with a sense of curiosity.
- Now bring this attention to your legs, then your abdomen, lower back, chest, upper back, arms, hands, shoulders, neck and face. Each time spend 20 to 30 seconds noticing any sensations that are there, exploring and investigating without having to actively look for them.
- If you become aware of any tension in the body, see how it is if you "breathe into" it.
- As with all mindfulness practices, if at any time you notice your mind wanders, simply acknowledge where it has wandered to and then gently return it to the part of the body you intended to focus on.

The Embodied Brain

Take a moment to consider the following:

Three men incarcerated in an Israeli prison appeared before a parole board consisting of a judge, a criminologist and a social worker. Over the course of the day many cases were heard, including the three below. The three prisoners had each completed at least two-thirds of their sentences, but the parole board granted freedom to only one of them. Which one do you think it was, and why?

Case 1 (heard at 8:50 a.m.): An Arab Israeli serving a 30-month sentence for fraud.

Case 2 (heard at 3:10 p.m.): A Jewish Israeli serving a 16-month sentence for assault.

Case 3 (heard at 4:25 p.m.): An Arab Israeli serving a 30-month sentence for fraud.

This question is derived from a research study[12] which looked at 1100 parole decisions over a 12-month period, where one-third of the cases seen were approved but there was one key variable that the researchers found dramatically affected the probability of being paroled – time of day.

Prisoners who appeared early in the morning received parole about 70% of the time, while those who appeared late in the day were paroled less than 10% of the time. That is a staggering difference. When do you think the next highest probability times occurred? If you said after lunch or after a morning break, you would be correct. Post-morning break there was a 65% chance of parole; before the break your chances were 20%; after lunch the probability was 60% (Figure 7.3).

When you are making decisions your brain is using glucose to provide the cognitive energy to make those decisions. A study in Miami[13] found that when people engaged in even a simple verbal fluency task, their glucose demands increased by 23%.

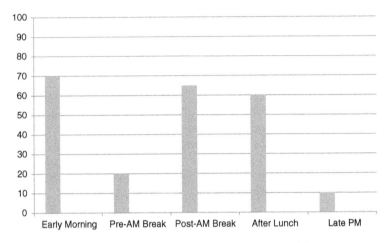

Figure 7.3 Percentage chance of parole in relation to time of day.

Making decisions is energy dependent – it requires glucose, and after each decision is made the resources available to make the next one are lower. There is a cumulative fatigue to making decisions, known as *"decision fatigue"*. When decision fatigue sets in, the brain has to make decisions with fewer resources, so it is here that simple, quick and easy decisions are sought, where biases and mental shortcuts are more likely, and where errors can occur. When the parole board was experiencing decision fatigue, the result was that their brains made the simplest of the two possible decisions – keeping prisoners incarcerated. At the start of the day, and following the morning break and lunch – when the parole board members had eaten and *rested* – their brains were *fuelled up* and their cognitive capacity improved, and so putting more thought and effort into a decision was possible.

The key finding is that rest and glucose impact our ability to make decisions. Daniel Kahneman, in his book *Thinking Fast and Slow*,[14] talks about how people often make their worst analytical decisions immediately before meals, when their glucose levels are most depleted. Roy Baumeister, author of *Willpower: Rediscovering Our Greatest Strength*,[15] suggests that because of this impact of energy on our brain function, good decision making is not a stable trait but fluctuates, and that: *"Even the wisest people won't make good choices when they're not rested and their glucose is low."*

When it comes to trading with the body in mind, it is not just intuition and gut feel that have an important impact on your trading decisions but also your energy levels. The mind is an energy system and it sits within the physical body, which is an energy system; changes in the body's energy levels affect your brain's performance. Energy has a direct impact on your brain's ability to make decisions and execute your trading strategy effectively – it is, in its own right, an edge.

Another resulting impact of low glucose levels is the impact on your self-control, what we would probably call in trading terms *discipline*. Studies[16] show that taxing mental and physical activities deplete glucose reserves and reduce our capacity for self-control. From an evolutionary perspective, the allocation of *resources* works on a last in, first out basis, with the thinking brain (neocortex) becoming the first to suffer.

The impacts of mental and physical fatigue are verifiably significant, and whilst many traders intuitively might know this, only a few have taken the steps to actively embrace it and to make it integral in their trading performance.

A summary of the impact of fatigue on decision making highlights several key points:

- The adoption of low-effort strategies – at the extreme, not trading at all.
- Cognitive ease – reduced high-level thinking and greater risk of bias.
- Quicker, less well thought out decisions.
- Impaired risk perception.
- Weighting of decision towards minimum effort for action.
- Reduced self-control.
- Increased risk of error.

In the longer term, fatigue has an impact on your health and on levels of commitment and motivation. It also affects your trading decision behaviour, moving you towards risk aversion. As famous American football coach Vince Lombardi once stated: *"Fatigue makes cowards of us all."*

Managing Energy, Becoming a Trading Athlete

Many trading floors have a culture of long working hours and the demands of trading are high emotionally, mentally and physically. However, as traders, disconnecting mind and body, ignoring signs of fatigue and ill-health and keeping going will affect your trading decisions and performance in the short term and your health and well-being in the long term. Managing energy should be seen as a priority for all traders, and for those who manage them.

Figure 7.4 shows some suggested ways in which you can manage your energy effectively and reduce mental and physical fatigue and its subsequent impact upon your trading decisions.

Sleep

A study[17] involving 29 young, healthy volunteers required them to undertake a variety of gambling-based tasks following a night without sleep. When the volunteers were rested they demonstrated typically cautious patterns of gambling behaviour, but with sleep deprivation their risk perception shifted and they became less sensitive to negative outcomes (losses) and put greater emphasis on positive outcomes (winning). The scientists at Duke University in North Carolina, where the study was conducted, used brain image scanning to monitor the volunteers' brain responses. *"Sleep deprivation surely makes gambling even more tempting to many people"* said

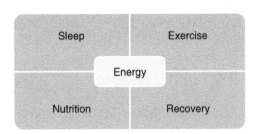

Figure 7.4 The four key components of managing energy.

Professor Scott Huettel. Vinod Venkatraman, the lead author of the study (published in the *Journal of Neuroscience*) said: "*Late-night gamblers are fighting more than just the unfavourable odds of gambling machines. They are fighting a sleep-deprived brain's tendency to implicitly seek gains while discounting the impact of potential losses.*" Professor Michael Chee of Duke University said: "*Even if someone makes very sound financial decisions after a normal night of sleep, there is no guarantee that this same person will not expose you to untoward risk if sleep deprived.*"

As well as affecting your risk preferences, sleep is key to cognitive functioning and has an impact on your ability to make intuitive judgements. A lack of sleep reduces glucose metabolism in the area of the brain correlated with sensing the environment that informs intuitive decision making; sleep-deprived individuals are less able to compare their current situation with past experiences and formulate appropriate decisions.[18] Sleep deprivation also affects your ability to concentrate.

Many traders I work with, and this has been a growing trend over the years, tell me how they feel sleep deprived, or do not sleep well. Some have to stay up late, or wake up in the early hours of the morning to make or receive calls from colleagues working in different time zones. Others have developed disrupted sleep patterns as a result of the general stresses and pressures of the trading environment. This is not just a problem in trading however, with research from the National Sleep Foundation in the USA[17] showing that as many as one-third of people may have sleep issues such as falling asleep, or staying asleep, and about 1 in 10 report some form of regular insomnia. Over half of these people put the blame on stress and worry.

Mindfulness-based approaches can be used to help you improve your sleep, and I have used such approaches with a number of my clients with positive results. A study conducted at Stanford Medical Centre[19] carried out a 6-week programme of mindfulness and cognitive behavioural therapy approaches with a group of 30 insomniacs. Following the programme, the attendees were able to get to sleep twice as quickly – taking 20 minutes as opposed to 40 – and approximately 60% of them no longer qualified as insomniacs. In a 12-month follow-up study they found that the majority of the benefits had remained. Another programme[20] at the University of Massachusetts Medical School developed an effective sleep therapy that incorporated meditation as an integral component and, in a non-controlled study of 102 insomniacs, 58% reported significant improvements and 91% of those using medication either reduced their dose or eliminated it completely. Six months later, 60% of respondents said the benefits had been maintained.

Developing your mindfulness through the practices alone will potentially help you with your sleep challenges as you begin to learn to observe your thoughts and emotions with greater awareness and get better at managing your mind. One of the outcomes of the work done with US Marines was that the soldiers from the study reported sleeping better following their mindfulness training.

Practice: Mindful Sleep

Many people who have sleep challenges find themselves either not falling asleep quickly or waking up and then being unable to fall back to sleep. One of the contributing factors to this can be people's propensity to evaluate and analyse why they are awake, or have woken up, and the stream of cognitive activity that ensues actually keeps them awake.

You can use mindfulness to help with your sleeping in two ways:

- Do some mindful breathing or a body scan, both of which will help you to relax.
- When you find your mind analysing, or wandering to other matters, simply acknowledge where it has gone and then bring it gently back to the breath or body. This process will help you to reduce the "wake-up" effect induced by your problem-solving mind.

Exercise

Countless studies have consistently shown the benefits of exercise in terms of its effect on our mood, ability to focus and to manage stress. Exercise increases oxygen flow into the brain, which is accompanied by a rise in mental sharpness. It also acts directly on the molecular machinery of the brain itself. It increases neurons' creation, survival and resistance to damage and stress. Recent research in neuroscience has reinforced the importance of exercise towards general brain health, its ability to reduce the effects of ageing upon the brain and its ability to help with the production of new neural pathways. Exercise releases growth factors in tissues and the brain that enhance neuronal growth and repair.

From a mindfulness angle, one form of exercise during the trading day could come from a mindful walk. Walking is an excellent way to exercise and relieve stress; it is also a good booster of mood. Taking a walk during the trading day can help you to get perspective on the markets and your performance. If the walk can be outside, then even better. Walk slowly, focus your awareness on the contact between feet and ground, notice the movement of your muscles and tendons, feel the motion of walking. Pay attention to the sights, sounds and smells around you.

Another alternative and mindfulness-friendly approach to exercise could come in the form of some mindful movement, yoga or tai-chi. All of these require minimal equipment, space or time and can even – where appropriate – be performed near to your trading desk.

You can also bring a mindful approach to your regular exercise regime, as demonstrated in the *Treadmill Practice* below.

Practice: Mindful Exercise – The Treadmill

Here is an example of how you can bring mindfulness training to exercising. The benefits of this include doubling the outcomes from each workout – mental and physical – and connecting your mind and body.

- Before you start your exercise session take a moment and state your intention for the session you are about to undertake.
- Warm up as usual, and progressively build up to your required pace.
- Now turn your awareness to your breath. Count on each exhale, moving from 1 through to 10. When you get to 10, start again.
- If your mind wanders from the breath, simply observe where it has wandered to, acknowledge it and bring your attention back to your breath.
- Continue this process for the duration of your exercise session.

When you start to do this practice you may wish to incorporate it in short doses to begin with, perhaps starting with 5 minutes during a session, before increasing your time as you progress.

Nutrition

Nutrition provides glucose to the body and brain and, as we saw from the prison parole board study, its impact on your ability to make decisions is significant. Key nutritional pointers are to ensure that you start the day with breakfast to get fuel into the system, and then eat regularly throughout the day to manage your insulin and glucose supplies. Generally, fruits and grains provide a slower and more efficient release of energy than simple sugars such as chocolate and sweets. Keeping an awareness of your energy levels throughout the day is a key part of being mind fit, which can be achieved by *checking in* regularly and asking *"how am I feeling now?"* Have an awareness of your *crucial moments* in terms of energy levels through the trading day and manage these as best you can.

Practice: Nutritional Mindfulness

Here are a couple of very simple ways in which to bring an element of mindfulness to your nutritional approach.

Body Check
Check in with your body's energy levels. Is it tired? Are you thirsty? Are you hungry? Do one thing to give your body some respite.

Hydrate
Pour yourself a glass of water. Enjoy the sound of it pouring into the glass. Go off and drink it some place. Do nothing else.

Eat
Eat lunch silently and slowly today. Look at what's at the end of your cutlery. Appreciate it. It will taste better.

Rest and Recovery

In his book *Stress for Success*,[21] James Loehr places great emphasis on the need for recovery. He states that: *"Either too much stress without recovery or too much recovery without stress ultimately becomes dysfunctional."* He refers to periods of stress and recovery, of activity and rest, as oscillation – a cycle – that is key to peak performance and in opposition to linearity. Linear stress leads to energy depletion in the muscles, adrenal glands, endocrine system and nervous system, and to the build up of the stress hormone cortisol, which can have, as will be discussed at more length later in the book, profound effects on your trading behaviour and physical health.

Circadian rhythms are your body's 24-hour cycle and are part of a myriad of cycles known as basic rest–activity cycles (BRAC) that impact your energy, mood, alertness, emotional state, strength, resistance to disease and performance. When we disturb our natural rhythms of activity and rest, psychobiology researcher Ernest Rossi suggests we become vulnerable to disturbances in our performance and health. Rossi introduces the idea of *"ultradian rhythms"* (Figure 7.5)[22] – cycles of 90–120 minutes of *stress* (activity) followed by 15–20 minutes of *recovery* (rest) – and states the importance of the recovery phase, particularly in avoiding depletion of glucose and insulin. Where possible, making a conscious effort to take some rest every 90–120 minutes could prove very beneficial. This "rest" could involve something as simple as having some fruit to eat, getting a glass of water, standing up and stretching, taking a short mindful walk, practising some mindful breathing, or a combination of any of these dependent on the market activity, time of day and general appropriateness. Be aware of your mind's temptation to refute such ideas and keep you chained to the desk in fear of missing out. Much of what we have discussed can be practised within arm's reach of your mouse, and longer and more distant breaks can be planned during times when you know the market is less likely to be busy. Finding time to switch off is essential in order to be fully able to switch on. Balancing your sympathetic nervous system (the fight or flight response) with the parasympathetic nervous system (rest and digest) is key, and a failure to get the balance right – to be *on* too much and *off* too little – can lead to *"sympathetic dominance"*, which results in adverse effects on your energy systems, brain function and trading performance.

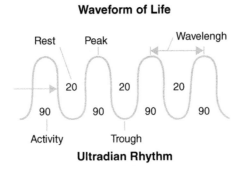

Figure 7.5 Ernest Rossi's ultradian rhythms.

A commitment to energy management can play a significant role in reducing fatigue and enhancing your trading decisions and performance, and is all part of becoming more mindful and developing mind fitness.

Putting It All Together

Key to managing your energy is knowing yourself – awareness. Developing an awareness of your own unique energy patterns, mapping them out and then looking at ways in which you can utilise them within your trading. Try to figure out when you are at your best, and when you are at your worst; when your *energy level crucial moments* are and what effective action you will take to manage them. Be mindful, pay attention to your energy levels, incorporate mindfulness into your sleeping, exercising, eating and recovery as is useful and helpful for you.

Reconnecting

Your mind and body go back a long way. Over the years you may have inadvertently distanced them; you will not be alone in this. Now, though, is maybe the time to bring them back closer together, to act upon the compelling neuroscience research that is telling us what many of us probably knew already, that our mind and body are one integrated system, that when we tune in to our bodies we can be open to signals that indicate risks or opportunities, and can positively shape our decision-making behaviour.

8

Habits, Behaviour, Action

Action Creates Results

Think for a moment about this question – how do you make or lose money trading?

You can go into great intricacies and details about the methodologies you use, the decision processes you go through, the role of emotions, biases, thoughts, feelings, external factors and more, and ultimately what you will eventually come down to is action – pressing buttons, a behaviour. You cannot think a position into the market or think your way out of it, and you cannot feel yourself in or out of positions. To enter and exit positions requires action, you can only make or lose money through action. Of course, our actions, our behaviours, are influenced by our thoughts, emotions, urges and physical energy, however one of the central themes of this book is teaching you how to work with your emotions and feelings, and thinking processes, more effectively so that you can pursue the most skillful and effective action in any given situation – even in the midst of potentially disruptive emotions or thoughts. This is something that Gardner and Moore, in their book *The Psychology of Enhancing Human Performance,*[1] refer to as *"poise"*: *"The ability to act in the service of your values and goals despite 'negative' internal states such as thoughts, emotions and physical sensations that you may be experiencing." "The ability to experience distress and still function as needed."* This always reminds me of a parachute jump. Sitting at the door of the plane about to jump, with very strong emotions in play, a function of the stress response kicking in, thoughts of *"why am I jumping out of a perfectly good plane with just a rucksack and a piece of silk inside to get me down to earth?"*, an awareness of strong physical sensations within the body – increased heart rate, faster/shallower breathing, tight muscles, dry mouth, maybe some shaking in the hands. And with all of that going on, which is a perfectly normal response for any new jumper, people still jump. They are able to take committed and effective action even in the presence of potentially disruptive thoughts, emotions and physical sensations. There are many trading situations where similar experiences are encountered – the anxiety of holding on to a profitable trade, the fear of taking a loss, the hesitation over getting back into the market following a period of losses, or not trading when the markets are quiet and boredom sets in. All of these are normal trading situations, with quite normal – often referred to as primary or "clean" – responses, but for each situation the goal in trading is to be able to take the most effective or skillful action in that situation even when sometimes our thoughts and emotions at that time may make it difficult. Often the behavioural choice we make in the short term acts in opposition to the benefits we can get in the long term. Taking profits earlier reduces the feelings of anxiety now, but may be stopping you from maximising your profits in the longer term. Avoiding a loss avoids the pain of loss now, but opens you up to the potential of greater loss and pain in the future. Not entering the market now avoids the pain of another loss, but also stops you from being able to win. And so on (Figure 8.1).

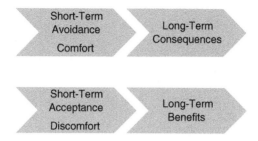

Figure 8.1 Enhancing your performance may require you to move from short-term avoidance and comfort to short-term acceptance and discomfort.

Reflection

What are you currently doing that is making your trading worse in the long run; keeps you stuck or wastes time or money; drains your energy; has a negative impact?

Habits – "Frighteningly Subtle, Incredibly Powerful"

Your behaviour is the result of your genetics, experience and environment (Figure 8.2). Each of these three components plays a part in shaping your brain, in developing the neural pathways (connections) within the brain that form the basis for your behavioural responses. Much of our behaviour becomes automatic, habitual, through repetition and the brain's focus on automating behaviour for energy efficiency. It is easier to "run" an old behavioural response than it is to create a new one. Much of our behaviour is simply a repeat of what we have done in the past – unless we make a conscious effort to change it. From this perspective, unlike the standard fund disclaimer *"past performance is not a predictor of future performance"*, when it comes to behaviour it is quite true to assume that *"past behaviour is a predictor of future behaviour"*.

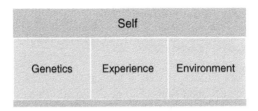

Figure 8.2 The three building blocks of "self".

Habits are, as Mark Williams states in his book, *"frighteningly subtle, yet can be incredibly powerful"*. Habits – your automatic reactions and responses – have evolved through repetition, through experience. Where, within the brain, you have created well-established neural pathways that enable you to repeat these actions, emotional and thinking responses without conscious effort. Learning to drive a car is a great example of how, through repetition and practice, the skills you learn become automated. Automating your responses and behaviours is an evolutionary process that allows the brain to extend your working memory, your ability to pay attention consciously and take conscious action in the moment – such as doing price calculations and weighing up options – whilst other processes operate beneath conscious awareness, with lower energy requirements. Automatic pilot therefore has many evolutionary advantages; however, it is possible for all of us to have automated some responses that may not be useful in optimising our market returns. Sometimes people refer to these as *"bad habits"*. I prefer to refer to them as outdated habits, or habits which no longer have utility (are not useful in the context of what you are trying to achieve). Your brain is always acting in your best interests. A behaviour you developed in the past may have given you some benefit and been useful to you *in the past*, but as you move through life and through your trading career, useful behaviours learnt in the past may no longer be useful in the present, as contexts such as markets, role and life events evolve. One example of this is a trader I coached who was having a challenge with scaling up his risk taking, even though he was a very capable and successful trader. When talking to him about his situation and what he was trying to achieve, he mentioned that in his early days of trading the institution he traded in – and his manager – were very risk focused and discouraged bigger trading positions. "*Big losses*" were actively discouraged. He had become an extremely tight manager of risk as a result of this experience and environment, but in his new environment he was subsequently finding it hard to take bigger risks as the thought of a potential big loss held him back. His very tight risk-taking approach that had got him success in his first trading role was now the very same behaviour that was holding him back.

Automatic pilot, then, is functional and useful, but being on automatic pilot consistently can lead to traders repeating patterns of behaviour that are detrimental to making the best decisions and achieving their performance. One of the benefits of mindfulness training is developing a greater awareness of your moment-to-moment experience and, through practice and over time, developing the ability not only to notice your habitual responses but also as a result being able to change them.

Building Patterns of Effective Action

Take a moment to fold your arms. Now pay attention to your own unique style of folding your arms. Notice how you might slide your hands under your upper arms, or they might be "gripping" or resting on them. Notice how your hands might be open or closed like a fist. Notice the amount of tension in your shoulders. Now, fold your arms so that they are completely the opposite way around. What do you notice?

For most people it takes conscious effort and time to do this. When they have eventually folded their arms the other way around it then feels very uncomfortable, and they want to go back to folding their arms the *normal* way.

Once you have a habit, like folding your arms, it takes time and effort to change it, and the feelings of discomfort of the *new* behaviour create an urge to return to the old way.

Developing any behaviour takes time and repetition – that is how the neural pathways in the brain are developed. Changing a behaviour takes even more time and effort, so it is really important to focus on building good trading behaviours, habits, to create neural pathways that provide automated responses to support effective trading performance.

Excellence is an art won by training and habituation. We do not act rightly because we have virtue or excellence, but we rather have those because we have acted rightly. We are what we repeatedly do. Excellence, then, is not an act, but a habit.

Aristotle

In the world of medicine, one significant shift in approach has been the move away from pathological models of healthcare – when they are ill, fix them – to preventative well-being approaches where time and money are invested at the *"front-end"* to reduce the frequency and intensity of illness and then treat whatever has to be treated beyond this. My view of trading is very similar, whereby traders can invest a little time and effort in developing good trading habits but should reasonably expect to experience a greater amount of *psychological* interference in their trading; or can invest more time and effort in developing effective behaviours and habits with the benefit that they will probably experience a reduced level of interference from their thoughts, emotions and feelings (although by the nature of market uncertainty and being human, they will still experience a certain amount of psychological challenge). The difference in the two approaches is represented in what I have termed the *"performance funnel"* (Figure 8.3), which can either be positive or negative. A positive funnel is one where the trader has developed their edge (defined in its broadest terms as anything that can provide a competitive advantage, so including energy, attention, etc.) through skills, knowledge, strategy and behaviours such that interference is sufficiently reduced. A negative funnel is one where a trader's edge is less developed and, as such, they experience a greater amount of interference within their trading of the markets.

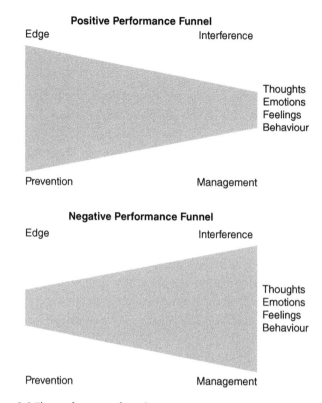

Figure 8.3 The performance funnel.

As a trader, developing your edge is not just about having a competitive strategic advantage, but also about maximising your opportunities and chances of success through your skills, knowledge, attitudes, physical state, emotional responses, attention and focus, for example. Small changes and improvements to your trading behaviour can – over the trading year and your career – make a significant difference. Recognising that small improvements can make a difference is very useful, as traders can sometimes fall into the trap of looking for the "big thing". This type of thinking is in line with an approach to developing high performance that has become common in elite sports and is known as the *"aggregation of marginal gains"* – looking for several areas that may add a small difference to performance (perhaps just 1%) and then *stacking* them to create more significant gains. Al Pacino, in the film *Any Given Sunday*,[2] delivers a rousing and inspirational speech to the American football team that he is coaching before the big game. This is known as the *"inches"* speech, and follows a similar theme of how small factors can make a difference to a result, and that the *inches* you need are all around you.

You find out life's this game of inches, so is football. Because in either game – life or football – the margin for error is so small. I mean, one half a step too late or too early and you don't quite make it. One half second too slow, too fast and you don't quite catch it. The inches we need are everywhere around us. They're in every break of the game, every minute, every second. On this team we fight for that inch. On this team we tear ourselves and everyone else around us to pieces for that inch. We claw with our fingernails for that inch. Because we know when we add up all those inches, that's gonna make the difference between winning and losing! Between living and dying! I'll tell you this, in any fight it's the guy who's willing to die who's gonna win that inch.

Excerpt from Al Pacino's "inches speech" from
Any Given Sunday.

Examples of "inches" to be found in trading might include:

- knowledge
- understanding
- skill
- speed
- systems
- preparation
- risk management
- behaviours and habits
- energy levels
- emotional responses
- perception
- ways of thinking about the markets
- sleep
- nutrition
- exercise
- recovery
- team support
- physical environment

- leadership
- culture
- resources and support
- coaching
- training
- evaluating and analysing trading performance
- mindfulness training.

One trader I coach, who has been very successful over a period of time, puts a lot of his success and consistency down to preparation. He has told me that on any given day in the markets, he feels that maybe only 30% of traders are fully prepared, and knowing that gives him a psychological edge. However, he has also told me how – by being prepared – he feels calmer in the markets, and that he is proactive (rather than reactive) to market events. Being prepared was an edge.

Another trader stated the importance of understanding what was going on in the markets before trading them, which for him added his edge. Other traders have stated the importance of feeling rested and energised, or of having strong downside risk management as edges.

A useful exercise to complete when looking at developing effective trading behaviours is to break your trading performance down into the three stages of performance (Figure 8.4) and for each section, think about what effective behaviours you would want to demonstrate in order to maximise your performance and market returns.

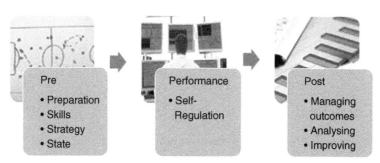

Figure 8.4 The three stages of performance.

Reflection

Take a moment to think about the type of trader you would like to be.

- *What behaviours would that trader demonstrate?*

- *Which of those behaviours do you have already?*

- *Which of those behaviours do you need to develop?*

- *Are there any behaviours that you need to let go of?*

Committed Action

There is a difference between knowing what action is effective and actually taking that action. The difference between knowing and doing can sometimes be down to psychological and biological processes such as thoughts, emotions, impulses and hormones – as we have explored in depth in this book already – but it can also be down to a lack of commitment to taking effective action. When I work with new traders they all tell me how motivated they are to become successful traders, and that they will do anything possible to achieve success. After a while, however, many fail to sustain or initiate some of the fundamental behaviours required. They may be motivated (wanting) to be successful traders, but they are not committed. *"Commitment is demonstrated when one regularly and consistently demonstrates the specific behaviours and activities that are directly related to optimal performance"*, as Gardner and Moore state.

One way of enhancing commitment is to move away from the idea of isolated behaviours and instead to begin to connect them to something stronger and more compelling – your purpose, goals and values. This sits them within a *higher power* and creates a stronger leverage on them (Figure 8.5).

Let's start by considering your trading values, what is important to you about trading and being a trader. Values provide a context for motivating changes and guiding courses of action. Values are a powerful driver of behaviour. In an article entitled "Shock exclusive: Top footballer refuses bribe" (*The Times*),[3]

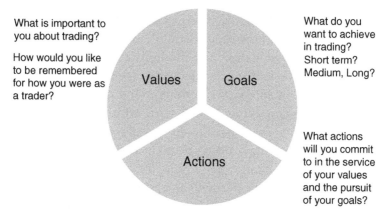

What is important to you about trading?

How would you like to be remembered for how you were as a trader?

Values

Goals

What do you want to achieve in trading? Short term? Medium, Long?

Actions

What actions will you commit to in the service of your values and the pursuit of your goals?

Figure 8.5 Leveraging effective action through commitment.

sportswriter Matthew Syed presents a case for learning from the people who refuse to cheat or take bribes in sport rather than always hearing from those who have. He states that: *"... contrary to economic orthodoxy, behaviour is not just about incentives, it is about values. We should not merely be asking how we can increase surveillance and punishment to deter criminals. We should also be asking how we bolster the values that enable societies (and sports) to function in the first place."* I have, on some courses I have run, taken the difficult step of asking traders to identify and reflect on their values, to think about the impact on their trading of holding such values – a concept I have called *"Values-Based Trading"*. Identify what is really important to you as a person and as a trader, and then use that to identify key behaviours and actions. In the banking sector, where *rogue trading* and *insider trading* cases have been high profile, looking not just at the incentives of trading floors but also at the values that underpin them may have real benefit in regulating traders' behaviour.

I witnessed the effectiveness of a values-driven approach within trading at a company offsite I attended of a very successful trading firm, where the CEO and founder of the group gave a presentation based around the importance of the company's values and of one core value in particular – professionalism. From a strong commitment to professionalism, he told everyone, we will get good performance and from good performance we will achieve profits. He then went on to provide clear behavioural examples of how people within the company were demonstrating professionalism and the impact that it was having on performance and the company's year-on-year increasing profitability. This approach is counter to the approach of many people and organisations, which starts with profits and then works back to what we have to do to achieve those profits. At a time when there have been several incidences of rogue trading, market manipulation and insider trading within the industry, traders' behaviour is heavily under scrutiny and banks and funds are keen to look to mitigate the risks of these incidences occurring. Building a strong values-based trading culture is one way in which that could be achieved. For the individual trader, a strong sense of your trading values and the behaviours that reflect them will generate greater commitment and adherence to those behaviours (Figure 8.6).

Figure 8.6 Values-based trading – building on the value of professionalism.

Take some time to complete the practice below to help you elicit your own values.

Practice: Eliciting Trading Values

Answering these questions may give you some insights into what your trading values are:

- *What matters to you in trading? What do you really want as a trader?*

- *What do you disapprove of or dislike in the actions of others? How would you act differently in their shoes?*

(continued)

- *Role model – think of someone who is a role model in trading for you. What inspires you about them? What are their strengths? What qualities and characteristics do they possess?*

- *What personal strengths and qualities do you already have? Which ones would you like to develop?*

- *How would you like to be thought of, seen or remembered as a trader?*

- *What behaviours would be consistent with a trader holding those values?*

Now consider the goals that you would like to achieve in trading, both in the long term and the shorter term. When you are thinking about goals you may like to use this adapted version of the SMART model to assist you. I like the inclusion of *"meaningful"* and *"adaptive"* in this particular model.

Write your goals down:

Specific – what specifically do you want to achieve?
Meaningful – guided by values, meaning, purpose.
Adaptive – moving you forward in the direction you want to go.
Realistic – realistically achievable with other demands.
Timed – day and date as far as possible.

Time Frame	Goal (s)
Long (2–5 years)	
Medium (1 year)	
Short (0–6 months)	

Figure 8.7 Driving committed action through values and goals.

Now, thinking about your values *and* your goals (Figure 8.7), what behaviours will you commit to that enable you to be true and consistent to your values and that will help you to move forward towards your goals?

Habit Releasing and Learning New Skills

As you develop an increasing awareness of your behaviours and habitual responses through your mindfulness practice, as well as being able to identify your effective habits and behaviours you will also no doubt come across behaviours and habits that are not as effective, that actually interfere with your trading decisions and performance. A useful perspective to take when it comes to behaviours and habits is to see them as skills. Taking losses is a skill. Not taking losses is a skill. The question is, which skills have you developed? I like the skills perspective because it can be a useful frame for viewing behavioural change; it reinforces the notion of development through practice, which is exactly how new behaviours are built. One trader I worked with found it very hard to get over a loss, dwelling on it for a long while, and he knew that this was not helpful for him, clouding his perception of the market. "*It sounds like you have developed the skill of dwelling to a high level*", I said, "*can you teach me how to dwell as well as you do? What do I have to do? What would the skill of not dwelling so much be like? How could you develop that skill?*"

Here are three approaches to help you let go of old behaviours and habits and develop new ones.

1 *Mindfulness of Behaviour*

Bring a sense of full awareness to the habit or behaviour that you want to release as you are doing it in the moment. Notice the thoughts, feelings, emotions and bodily sensations that are present. Bringing this sense of full awareness to the behaviour can help you to manage it, see it for what it is – an automated habitual reaction – and, if appropriate, let go of it.

2 *Habit Releasing*

Habit releasing is a popular part of mindfulness-based programmes and involves you in consciously bringing awareness to existing habits and then purposefully changing some of your habits, for example choosing to sit in a different chair to watch TV, or brushing your teeth with the opposite hand, or going for a deliberately slow walk with no destination in mind.

Practice: Habit Releasing

Here are some examples of habit-releasing practices to use:

- Choose a routine activity and make a deliberate effort to bring moment-to-moment awareness to it. This could be anything from making and drinking a cup of tea or coffee, to brushing your teeth, having a shower, walking to work; make sure that you are at the point of knowing what you are doing as you are doing it.
- Change the chair that you sit in to watch TV, or at the dinner table. See how a different location feels, and how your perspective changes.
- Change a part of your commute to work – the route of the drive or walk, or get off one stop earlier at the tube/underground. Change something, make it different.
- Go for at least one 15-minute or longer walk this week; walk slowly and mindfully, take a look around, open up your senses.

3   *Building a New Habit – Learning the New Skill*

When you want to let go of, or release, an existing habit you should give real consideration to what you are going to replace it with. Start by thinking about the situations when you would like to be doing the new behaviour. Then remind yourself of what your old approach was. Now, carefully and clearly decide on how you want to perform in the future. You can then use mental rehearsal or visualisation, processes used extensively in sports psychology, to imagine yourself in those situations performing your new behaviour. When you are visualising you are engaging the same neural circuitry within the brain as if you were performing the behaviour for real – the mind cannot tell the difference between a real and an imagined experience. This ability to practise in your mind, whilst developing neural pathways in the brain, is important in the fact that traders – unlike, say, athletes – have little time or facility for "practice" and events for rehearsing may be infrequent and so not provide enough repetition to develop the pathways in the brain in order to create the required change. I have used visualisation very successfully with traders on a number of occasions, generally where they have a very clearly identified behaviour they wish to develop in specific situations. For example, a trader who wanted to be able to get out of his trades at his stop loss more often; a trader who wanted to stop jumping back into the market following a losing trade; a trader who was about to increase his trading position size.

Practice: Mental Rehearsal

- Get into a comfortable seated position.
- Take a few moments to relax, perhaps by taking 10 very mindful breaths.
- Take your attention to imagining the situation you wish to perform your new behaviour in – imagine being there; see what you would see; hear what you would hear; feel what you would feel. Make it as real as you possibly can.

- Practise in your mind doing the behaviour you have decided to develop.
- Repeat the previous two steps between 2 and 5 times, depending on how long they take and how much time you have available.
- Bring your attention back to the room.

Flexible Response

No man ever steps in the same river twice, for it's not the same river and he's not the same man.

Heraclitus c. 535–475 BC

A theme that has been touched upon several times within this book is that of being flexible in your response to situations, of making decisions based on the situation that you are in. To do this requires good situational awareness, to be able to read the market environment you are in, and being mentally agile, to be able to adapt or change your thinking processes to it. To some degree, this goes against the old adage of *"have a plan and trade the plan"*. Having a plan is helpful in trading and adds much help psychologically when it comes to execution, however blindly sticking to the plan as markets change is not useful in maximising your returns. In the military there is a well-known maxim called the 7 Ps: "Proper Planning and Preparation Prevents Piss Poor Performance." *Preparation* with high attention to detail and what-if scenarios is very important. However, there is a second maxim: *"No plans survive first contact."* There is a need to be flexible according to changes in events and unforeseen factors, and this is just the same in trading. *"Every moment in the market is unique"*, so commit to effective action but remember that skillful effective action is situational, and flexible not rigid. As you gain experience and develop your judgement you will gain greater insights into what effective action is for a specific situation, it cannot always be predetermined. One way in which you can develop your judgement more quickly is through market scenario playback and rehearsal. Replaying past market situations and assessing your judgement calls, and then thinking about future market situations that could occur and how you would respond, helps to prime your brain's circuits for action. Your market returns will be a function of the quality of your judgement calls.

9

Turning Towards Difficulty

The Difficulties of Trading

Trading, as we have seen, presents traders with many challenges and difficulties – decision making under conditions of uncertainty, coping with the outcomes of those decisions and their potential consequences, performing in an extremely results-driven environment, managing relationships and dealing with change. When traders encounter big losses, extended losing runs, changes in market conditions, institutional restructuring, stressful life events or other challenges, how they respond to these events is a determinant of the impact that they will have on their trading performance. You cannot control the events that happen to you, you can only control your response to them (Figure 9.1). One of the key psychological qualities required for successful trading is resilience – the ability to deal with, and respond effectively to, the events and challenges that trading the markets brings and the feelings of stress that may come from them. One of the core outcomes of the mindfulness-based approach presented in this book is to help you to develop the resilience required to trade the financial markets.

E + R = O (Events + Responses = Outcomes)

Figure 9.1 It is not the events that happen to us that matter, rather how we respond to those events.

Stress, Pressure and Trading Performance

You are sitting at your trading desk as some key and anticipated data, perhaps non-farm payrolls, are released and you see the market react, your heart quickens, breathing increases, muscles tense and stomach knots up. Your body is preparing, your stress response has been activated.

The stress response is designed primarily to help you assess and respond to danger, to a perceived threat. It is an evolutionary survival mechanism which, in its early beginnings, was used to help you get out of physical danger, the threat of the sabre tooth tiger and other such animals. Today the triggers for the stress response (stressors) are very different indeed, not so much physiological as psychological, yet the response is the same. A sharp move in the market, your position going offside, a losing trade, all of these can be perceived as a threat and can activate your stress response.

It is the amygdala (radars) in the limbic system (emotional centre) of your brain that is assessing for threats, and when one is detected, your *fight or flight* stress response is triggered, engaging the sympathetic nervous system. The initial response, the alarm response, sees your blood being flooded with adrenaline and cortisol, your heart rate and blood pressure increasing, your breathing quickening and your blood being directed quickly towards your muscles. Under *threat*, short-term *survival* is the priority and the allocation of the body's resources puts this over longer-term needs such as digestion, immune system function, growth and reproductive processes, which are shut down.

It is important to emphasise at this point that each individual has a unique stress response. Whilst the physiological mechanisms that come into play are the same for each of us, the sensitivity of our amygdala and the stressors that trigger the response are unique. Stress is often viewed as an external factor when it is, in fact, internal – stress is a perception. It is your perception of an event as a threat that will activate your fight or flight response, and this is, of course, very individual. We saw this earlier in the book, with the example of the trader who heads up a desk in a bank where heavy regulation and associated changes are creating high demands on the team. Most of the team see these events as threatening and *negative* and experience symptoms of stress accordingly. The head of desk, however, has a different perception. He sees these events as leading to a big opportunity for his bank to grab a bigger share of the market as smaller competitors are eventually squeezed out by the costs of updating systems, processes and staff. The events are the same, but the perception as either a threat or an opportunity will determine the physiological responses and the psychological experience. Your stress response is a function of genetics, environment and experience and can be modified over time as a result and reduced in sensitivity – it can be trained (Figure 9.2).

In the short term and in short bursts, stress is performance enhancing, but too much stress over too long a period, especially when it is above your ability to cope with, has the potential to be extremely damaging mentally and physically. Figure 9.3 illustrates the effects of levels of stress on performance in an inverted-U relationship based on the Yerkes–Dodson curve developed in 1908.[1] Too little perceived stress and performance is low. This can be seen when traders are faced with quiet market conditions, or are taking very little risk – boredom and complacency can creep in. Too much stress and performance is again low. This

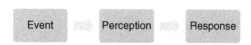

Figure 9.2 The role of perception in the stress response.

Figure 9.3 The stress–performance inverted-U curve.

is typical of extremely volatile market conditions or when traders are taking big risk positions, where traders can experience increased feelings of anxiety. At the top of the curve is the *zone of optimal performance*, and this is where your performance is likely to be at its best – the level of demand and challenge from the markets are matched to your capabilities and perceived ability to cope.

When stress is acutely high or extends over a prolonged period of time, you can start to experience detrimental effects. An extended losing run or a period of prolonged change or excessive challenge can all result in you experiencing what is called *"chronic stress"*.

Chronic stress has a very damaging impact on trading performance, with potential effects including:

- A depletion of cognitive, physical and mental reserves.
- A bias towards reactive or emotional decision making.
- Disturbed sleep.
- Chronic pain.
- Cardiac complications.
- Gastrointestinal difficulties.
- Hypertension (high blood pressure).
- Immune system dysfunction.

- Increased feelings of anxiety.
- Depression.
- Substance abuse.
- Increased pessimism.
- Risk-aversive trading behaviour.

From a brain perspective, the effects of chronic stress include:

- A reduction in the amount of resources available for your prefrontal cortex; cognitive functions.
- Inhibited memory and learning processes.
- The engagement of more automated processes to reduce cognitive load; making decisions with fewer resources to use less energy and an increased risk of bias and error.
- Greater sensitivity to threat in the amygdalae.
- As anxiety and arousal increase, your focus moves inwards and you are more likely to miss external stimuli around you.

This longer-term exposure to stress leads to a state which was described in John Coates's book[2] as "*irrational pessimism*", underpinned by high levels of cortisol within the body, leading to traders becoming hypersensitive to threat and risk in the present, selectively recalling threatening episodes from the past and projecting more danger ahead in the future. In such a biological state it is not hard to see how this translates into risk aversion in a trader's behaviour. In the extreme, traders can experience symptoms of depression, exhaustion and numbness, like being "*stuck on low*". At the other end of the extreme, they can become "*stuck on high*" with insomnia, hyper-arousal and feelings of agitation and restlessness. As a trader, having a feel for your current levels of stress can be very useful, and the *Stress Barometer* practice can help you achieve this.

Being able to cope with the demands of trading is, in part then, a function of the sensitivity of your stress response to your perception of events and your range and effectiveness of coping strategies. It is dependent on your level of resilience.

Practice: The Stress Barometer

This practice is designed to help you develop a greater awareness of your physical feelings of stress, developing your own barometer:

- Determine a part of your body – chest, abdomen or somewhere in between the two – that you feel is sensitive to feelings of stress.
- Let this place become your "stress barometer" – a place where you can pay attention to the sensations that arise throughout the day.
- As you do this over time, and become more practiced, you will develop a greater awareness of the more subtle variations of feelings within this area.

Source: Adapted from *The Mindful Workplace*, Michael Chaskalson.

Resilience, Trader Toughness and Mind Fitness

In the *Oxford Dictionary*, resilience is defined as "the capacity to recover quickly from difficulties; toughness". Toughness is often cited as being an important quality for success in trading. The term "mental toughness" is commonly used in sporting and performance-based environments, but words such as *resilience* or *hardiness* are also used. Dr Suzanne Kobasa of City University, New York is a leading researcher and writer on hardiness and suggests that there are three psychological traits which are key to this characteristic – control, challenge and commitment.[3] During his 8-week Mindfulness-Based Stress Reduction programme at the University of Massachusetts Medical School, Jon Kabat-Zinn's team decided to investigate the impact of mindfulness training on hardiness – and the finding was that mindfulness training boosts hardiness. Practising mindfulness increases resilience and develops toughness. The research group reported feeling happier, more energised and less stressed; they felt more in control of their lives and were more able to see challenges as opportunities rather than threats following their mindfulness training.[4]

Resilience reflects your ability to withstand the challenges, demands and stresses of an event or set of events and can be developed in three ways:

- Resilience to stress is built through a process of exposing people to stress and then allowing them to recover afterwards, initiating a process of adaptation often referred to as *adaptive toughness.*
- Skills can also be taught that help people to cope more successfully with the effects of stress – shifting the balance of challenge and coping capability.
- Specific mental training techniques can be taught that reduce a person's stress reactivity.

The mindfulness-based approaches in this book are powerful because they provide interventions at all three levels – through developing adaptive toughness by approaching your experience, whilst also reducing amygdala sensitivity via the mindfulness practices, and then providing a range of strategies and approaches that can be applied to cope with and reduce feelings of stress.

A key finding from Jha and Stanley's study with the US Marines was the lowered feelings of stress that the soldiers experienced after their mind fitness training. The use of mindfulness-based approaches to help people in banking and fund management to manage the challenges, pressures and stresses that they face is growing, as reported in an FT.com article with the headline "Mindfulness gives stressed out bankers something to think about".[5]

Practising mindfulness helps your body with its regulation of the stress response and its effects within your nervous system. This is particularly important following an *episode* of stress, where practising mindfulness techniques can help your body to recover from and regulate the effects of stress by completing the stress–activation cycle: following the sympathetic nervous system *fight or flight* with activation of the parasympathetic nervous system, your relaxation response (also known as *rest and digest*) slowing down your heart rate, lowering your blood pressure and slowing down your respiration. Activation of this rest and digest system is very restorative. A period of rest or recovery is critical to managing stress and to the development of resilience. When the stress response is not released the body becomes imbalanced, what is known as dysregulated. This cycle of activation and recovery is a core theme in Loehr's book *Stress for Success*. Loehr sees stress as essential to growth and development, and increased performance, but only when it is balanced with adequate periods of recovery. This is a process he calls *"oscillation"*, as we touched upon when looking at energy management. Indeed, he contends that it is not the stress itself that is the problem for most people, but rather a lack of recovery. Practising mind fitness provides this valuable recovery component.

People who practise mindfulness report feeling less stressed and more emotionally "balanced". A study in the *Journal of Health Psychology*[6] showed that mindfulness practice is not only associated with leading to feelings of being less stressed, but is also linked to decreased levels of the stress hormone cortisol. A key neurological reason behind this change in stress levels is that amygdala (threat radar) reactivity is reduced, making people less reactive to threat. A study at Stanford University found that an 8-week mindfulness course reduced the reactivity of the amygdala and increased activity in the prefrontal cortex, which helps to regulate emotions, and this subsequently reduced stress levels.[7] At Harvard University, a similar research programme found that following the mindfulness training there was actually a lower density of neurons in the amygdala and a greater density of neurons found in areas of the brain involved in regulating emotions.[8]

Mindfulness training also helps traders to manage difficult times by helping them to reappraise, to see them differently. Because the stress response is activated by a perceived threat, being able to make shifts in perception creates shifts in the activation of the stress response. By its very nature, viewing your experience in this moment – in a non-judgemental way – is already a process of reappraisal. However, as we have explored in previous situations, being able to actively change perception by asking, for example *"How else could I see this situation?"* or *"How could I see this event in a more useful way?"* can be very helpful. A shift from seeing a loss as a devastating event to one in which there might be some useful learning, or something to gain, can result in an entirely different emotional response. Likewise, seeing a mistake as a *failure* versus seeing it as a *learning opportunity*. Every loss or setback is an opportunity, of course, to build resilience, and on the flipside, every big win or winning run provides an opportunity to deal with overconfidence.

A great practice that I picked up and adapted from Mark Williams's *Mindfulness* book is how bringing a sense of appreciation to the here and now can help you manage the emotions and sensations that may be present during a difficult time. Below you will see the *Hunting for the Good Stuff* practice that is designed to bring an awareness to 5 to 10 things you are grateful for, or view as positive. In positive psychology, and in the resiliency programmes taught to the US military, they refer to the ability to find positives amongst difficult times as *"hunting for the good stuff"*. The use of the word *hunting* is very appropriate, as finding positives during a really challenging time will, as we have seen, not be automatic or easy; it will, however, be very beneficial.

Practice: Hunting for the Good Stuff

Take time to identify 5 aspects of your trading performance or wider life, as appropriate/useful (one for each finger of your hand). These could include things you are grateful for, small successes, progress you have made. If you want to challenge yourself, go for 10 and fill up the fingers of both hands. Make this a daily practice when times are tough.

Approaching vs. Avoiding

In an experiment conducted at the University of Maryland and published in 2001,[9] a group of students were asked to play a game which involved solving a maze puzzle. This was done by drawing a line with a pencil from the middle of the maze to the exit without taking the pencil off the page. Two groups of students were tasked with helping a cartoon mouse to get to safety in its mouse hole. One group of students worked on a maze where there was a delicious-looking piece of cheese in front of the mouse hole at the exit of the maze; this is a positive or approach-orientated puzzle. The other group's maze had no cheese but instead had a picture of an owl that was poised to swoop and capture the mouse at any given moment; this is a negative or avoidance-orientated puzzle.

The mazes were relatively simple, with average completion time around 2 minutes, but there was a very interesting difference in the after-effects of the students. After completing the maze task the students were asked to complete a number of different tasks that measured their creativity. Those who had avoided the owl did 50% worse than those who had helped the mouse to find the cheese. Avoidance had *closed down* options in the students' minds, it had triggered their aversion pathways, leaving them with a lingering sense of fear and enhanced vigilance and caution. This had the result of reducing their creativity and flexibility. The cheese group, in contrast, were open to new experiences, playful, carefree, less cautious and more willing to experiment.

When your brain's aversion system is activated you will narrow your focus, be less creative, more anxious and less flexible. If you can activate its approach system, you can, of course, have the opposite experience.

Your brain's approach system is sensitive to potential rewards, and the risk avoidance system keeps us alert to threats. Professor Richard Davidson has shown that the approach system correlates to left prefrontal cortex activation in the brain and is associated with *positive* emotions, whilst our avoidance system correlates to the right prefrontal cortex area of the brain and is associated with emotions such as fear, anxiety and disgust and can inhibit movement towards our goals.[10] From an evolutionary perspective it is easy to see the value of these two systems. However, when combined with dispositional factors they can become skewed and some people might find that they have developed an overactive avoidance system, leading to greater feelings of anxiety, worry and stress. Interestingly, from a situational, environmental perspective, traders experiencing long periods of drawdown or challenges and change may find their balance shifting towards the avoidance system.

Davidson, along with Jon Kabat-Zinn, provided an 8-week mindfulness training programme to a group of workers at Promega – a high-pressure biotech business in Wisconsin – whilst a comparison group of workers received no training at all. Both groups were tested before and after the programme and some interesting outcomes evolved and were published in an article they wrote for *Psychosomatic Medicine* in 2003.[11] Prior to the study many workers at Promega were feeling highly stressed and were tipped towards the avoidance system. Following the mindfulness study what they reported was that their moods had improved, they felt more energised and engaged, and less anxious. Brain scans revealed that their left-to-right activation ratio had shifted significantly towards the left – they were activating more of the approach system. Significantly, these results were still valid at a 4-month follow-up. Mindfulness-based training helps your brain to engage more of its approach system, helping you to reduce the risk of straying too far towards irrational pessimism and the effects of chronic stress, and enabling you to cope with, and perform under, difficult times more effectively.

Exposure and Adaptive Toughness – Shifting the Curve

When you take an approach-based psychological path there are many benefits, both to your in-the-moment experience and also to what happens beyond that. By actively engaging and working with your thoughts, emotions and feelings in the moment, as is encouraged in mindfulness training, you are exposing yourself to them – the opposite of avoiding them – and in this process of exposure you are learning how to be with them, manage them and still take skillful and effective action. The more you expose yourself to these difficult situations, the more you develop your abilities to cope with and manage them – you build your *"stress capacity"*. This process of toughening that occurs as a result of meeting your difficult thoughts, emotions/feelings and experiences head on is know as *"adaptive toughness"* and works in much the same way as a muscle exposed to the stress of exercise grows stronger (providing that sufficient recovery is provided for the adaptation to occur).

This exposure effect was demonstrated in a study conducted by Andrew W. Lo and Dmitry V. Repin,[12] which showed that traders with a greater level of experience have lower levels of stress reactivity to market volatility than less experienced traders. Over their years of trading the markets – and through exposure to volatility, losses, change and other market stressors – the traders had adapted and reduced their stress response to such events. This reduction in sensitivity to the stress response, or increase in stress capacity as Loehr calls it, can be represented by a shift in the stress–performance curve (Figure 9.4), extending the zone of optimal performance.

It is important to note that this toughening process, just like training a muscle, is a two-part process. Firstly there is the

Figure 9.4 Adaptive toughness – shifting the curve.

exposure phase, when the muscle is worked, and then critically there is the recovery phase, when the muscle is rested and the adaptation occurs. Exposure to stress with sufficient recovery results in adaptation, an increased stress capacity and improved resilience. Exposure to stress with insufficient recovery results in breakdown and burnout.

Burnout and the Exhaustion Funnel

Stress without sufficient recovery results in breakdown, chronic stress and eventually, over time, what has often been termed "burnout". Being in a state of high arousal over time leaves traders *adrenal depleted* and feeling exhausted, resulting ultimately in risk-aversive behaviour. As we have discussed previously, it is not so much exposure to stress that is the problem, but rather a lack of recovery from it. In mindfulness teaching, the exhaustion funnel (Figure 9.5), developed by Professor Marie Åsberg from the Karolinska Institute, Stockholm,[13] is a popular model that is used to demonstrate the potential impact of high demands with insufficient recovery.

Traders who are watching price action tick-by-tick are particularly susceptible to stress and burnout, with the effects of volatility, enduring price swings in their favour and against them for hours and hours each day, week after week. For traders in these environments, measures to manage physical energy and ensure sufficient recovery in the short term and over time are absolutely critical.

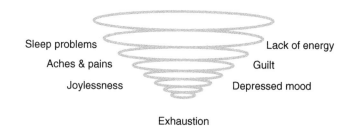

Sleep problems   Lack of energy
Aches & pains   Guilt
Joylessness   Depressed mood

Exhaustion

Figure 9.5 The exhaustion funnel.

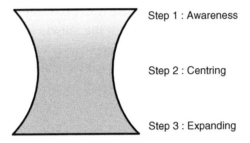

Step 1 : Awareness

Step 2 : Centring

Step 3 : Expanding

Figure 9.6 The 3-minute breathing space.

Practising mindfulness activates your parasympathetic nervous system, your relaxation response; it completes the stress–activation cycle by providing the important recovery element that allows your body and mind to adapt and become more resilient. A great mind fitness practice to use at times when you are feeling stress or fatigue is the *3-Minute Breathing Space*. The breathing space is a three-step process of firstly becoming aware of your experience in this moment, then bringing your awareness in to the breath before expanding your awareness back out to the whole body. The changing focus of awareness can be represented by an hourglass shape (Figure 9.6). The acronym ACE is a useful way of remembering the breathing space, as detailed in the practice box.

Practice: 3-Minute Breathing Space

Step 1. *Awareness*

Bring an awareness to this moment.

What *thoughts* do you have? Put them into words. See them as mental events "*My mind is thinking...*"

What *feelings* do you have? Turn towards them. "*I have the feeling of...*"

What *bodily sensations* do you have? Scan your body and acknowledge any sensations present.

Step 2. *Centring*

Now redirect your awareness to your breathing.

Bring your awareness to the physical sensations of breathing, perhaps a focus on your abdomen and its rise and fall with each breath.

Step 3. *Expanding*

Expand your awareness to get a sense of the whole body, including posture and facial expression.

If you become aware of any discomfort or tension, breathe into and out of it.

Become aware of the sounds around you, and your surroundings.

Bring this expanded awareness with you into this moment.

Mindfulness training is also very useful for dealing with stress, exhaustion and difficult times because it enables you to develop an awareness of your patterns of stress and fatigue, and the powerful negative spirals that can result. By turning towards them and observing them, you can begin to dissipate them.

One study[14] found that even as little as 10 minutes of mindfulness practice per day, 5 days a week for 4 weeks could result in a lowering of the symptoms of burnout, enhanced feelings of relaxation and improved life satisfaction. Another study looked at two companies that had introduced mindfulness to their employees, and reported a significant reduction in health problems, improved sleep and a reduction in the use of cigarettes and alcohol – which can often be used as coping mechanisms for stress.[15]

Turning Towards Difficulty

The ultimate measure of a person is not where they stand in moments of comfort and convenience, but where they stand at times of challenge. The most glorious moments in your life are not the so-called days of success, but rather those days when you dig deep and rise to face a challenge head on.

When faced with any kind of difficulty, the choice becomes to either approach it or attempt to avoid it. Difficulties are a part of trading; it is how you handle them that matters. For most people, trying to avoid or push away from difficult events is the norm, however, as we have seen, an approach focus has many more benefits for traders. Becoming more aware of your thoughts, emotions, feelings and bodily sensations evoked by these events gives you the possibility of moving away from your habitual automatic ways of reacting and towards more mindful effective responding. Turning towards a difficult situation has two key steps:

1 Notice your temptation to drive away or suppress thoughts, feelings, emotions and bodily sensations that you may deem *negative*; this is your aversive reaction.
2 Be open to them, approach them.

One way of developing an alternative method to deal with and relate to difficult challenges is to bring an awareness to the body. This idea is the theme of the next mind fitness practice, *Exploring Difficulty*.

Practice: Exploring Difficulty
- Start by getting yourself into a comfortable sitting position.
- Bring your attention to the sensations of your breathing, before widening your awareness to the whole body and then to sounds and thoughts (allow a few minutes for this).
- Bring to mind a difficulty or a concern that you want to explore.

- Once this troubling situation or thought has been brought to mind, allow it to rest there whilst bringing your attention to any physical sensations within the body that are occurring alongside it.
- Next, deliberately move the focus of your attention to the part of your body where the physical sensations are the strongest. Bring an awareness to this part of the body by "breathing into" it on the in breath and "out of it" on the out breath.
- Bring a sense of curiosity to the sensations that are there, exploring them as they come and go in that moment. Be open to them, allow them, approach them.
- As you stay with these sensations, notice your relationship with them. Are you trying to, or wanting to, get rid of them or are you able to give your full attention to them?
- When you notice that the bodily sensations are no longer pulling your attention to the same degree, simply return your focus to the breath.

Being willing to turn towards difficulty and embrace the thoughts and feelings that go with it is, although counterintuitive for many, a very useful approach – especially when dealing with losses and change. When traders take a significant loss, sustain continued losses or face change, their initial reactions are often shock and disbelief. Following this it is not unusual for traders to experience emotion-filled periods of anger and frustration and to look for people, events or causes to blame. These, according to the Kubler-Ross cycle (Figure 9.7), are a part of the normal process of coping with such events and precede a person being able to reach a point of acceptance of their situation, being able to let go, at which point only are they able to start to refocus, rebuild and move forward. Of course, every trader's reaction to an event will be determined both by the individual circumstances of the event and the individual nature of the trader themselves. With this model in mind, it is evident that getting to acceptance is a key point in the process, and in order to be able to do so traders must deal with the arising emotions that occur following the event. This is most effectively achieved, as we have discussed in earlier chapters and in this one, by being

Psychological Reactions to Change

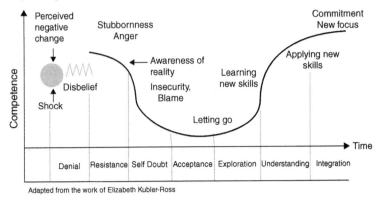

Adapted from the work of Elizabeth Kubler-Ross

Figure 9.7 The Kubler-Ross change cycle.

open to these thoughts and feelings, approaching them and working with them. An attempted suppression of these feelings and thoughts does not allow them to be processed and worked through; instead it contains them, they linger, often increasing in intensity and in doing so increasing the risk of acting them out in the future with potentially dire consequences.

Effective Action for Difficult Times

During a period of extended challenge or stress, managing yourself, your experience and your actions is key. How you experience this period and how you perform – both during it and after it – is dependent upon the choices that you make.

One trader I coached, let's call him Andy, had been offered coaching by his institution to help him with his performance following a period when his P&L had fallen quite a way below his expected budget for the year, following a difficult time the year before. When he came to coaching his mood was very low; in a long and successful career at several other banks it was the first time that he had ever been regarded as *underperforming*. The core of his underperformance was primarily down to a major shift in market conditions and, although he had tried to adapt to them, there was simply not much opportunity available and whilst his performance relative to market opportunity was probably quite high, in absolute terms he was not meeting the required benchmarks. Through the coaching we explored ways of optimising his trading strategies and approaches, but a major theme was also ensuring that his mood and mindset were managed such that should opportunities appear, he was ready to take them. Your mood and performance are related. To do this we focused on looking at effective action in this "difficult times" context, actions that would be enhancing of mood or mindset. The challenge at such times is that sometimes there is low motivation to take what might be considered effective action. When mood is low, motivation is also often low. This requires a reversal of the motivation process, a taking of action in order to boost motivation. In these times, motivation follows action (Figure 9.8).

When undergoing a particularly difficult time, with stress and exhaustion evident, it can be very helpful to combine the use of the *Breathing Space* practice presented above with effective action.

At times when you really notice feelings of stress or exhaustion, take a moment to practise your breathing space and follow it up with the question: *"What do I need to do for myself right now?"*

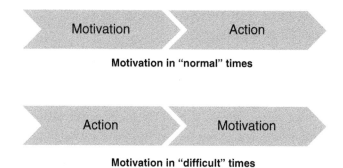

Figure 9.8 The reversal of the motivation process.

In terms of effective action for this particular context you have three options:

- Do something pleasurable.
- Do something that will give you a sense of satisfaction or mastery.
- Continue acting mindfully.

Do Something Pleasurable

When times are very tough, with extended drawdown and losing runs for example, the feelings of stress and exhaustion (and the low mood that often accompanies them) can leave traders in a state of "*anhedonia*" – where there is little feeling of enjoyment or pleasure. When the going gets tough, many traders work harder and longer – often at the expense of *nourishing* and restorative activities. This could include doing an activity that you find enjoyable – such as a favourite hobby, exercising, spending time with friends, watching a movie, reading, anything that you find "nourishing". It could also include doing something to be kind to your body, which, under stress, can become *neglected*. This might include getting some extra sleep, exercising, yoga practice, taking a walk or having a massage. In the case of Andy, he was a keen sailor and so made an extra effort to get some time in on the water at the weekends, and to spend more time with his family. He really found this helpful over the 3 months that we worked together. What would be on your list?

Do Something That Will Give You a Sense of Satisfaction or Mastery

When traders are anxious, stressed and exhausted it is not uncommon to see them losing a sense of control and purposefulness and becoming more *helpless*. When we feel out of control in one area of our life, it is possible for it to spread over into other areas of our life, and vice versa. Whilst engaging in such activities can sometimes be seen as actually adding to the state of exhaustion rather than relieving it, they are very powerful and can be very helpful – but you should start off with small steps.

Actions here might include exercising or completing some tasks that you have been putting off for a while, making something or DIY, or learning something new – whether it be knowledge or a skill, either trading related or not. What activities give you a sense of satisfaction, mastery, achievement or control?

Continue Acting Mindfully

Periods of difficulty are a common time for me to introduce traders to mindfulness through coaching. During stressful and challenging times they can often find themselves over-thinking matters, trying to fight their way out of their situation, trying to get rid of the *unwanted* thoughts and feelings that are accompanying their experience and becoming less and less mindful, more reactive and less responsive. Typically, traders can find their minds dwelling on past *good times* and going into the future in anticipation and hope of a quick return to *better times*. Taking time to "check-in", to connect with your present-moment experience using the *1-Minute Mindfulness* or *Breathing Space* practices, is an excellent way to connect with and stay focused on the present. What can you do to be more mindful during difficult times?

Even small changes of behaviour, taking small steps of effective action, can have a big impact on how you feel. Remember the marginal gains philosophy from earlier – the inches add up. In doing so, you can begin to reduce your feelings of stress and exhaustion, increase your energy levels and make a shift away from irrational pessimism and the exhaustion funnel and towards optimal performance. The brain you trade with is the same brain that goes home with you in the evenings. What you do both in and out of trading is affecting your neurochemistry, your biology and your psychology, making you more or less risk averse, more or less likely to see opportunity in the markets, more or less likely to make money. In Andy's case, a combination of more time spent sailing, quality time with his family and daily mindfulness practice all helped him to manage his mood and his mindset through an extremely difficult time. It did not change the markets, but it did help him to trade those markets more effectively. In the second month of our coaching programme Andy was able to capture a couple of good moves in the market that left him only slightly beneath where his monthly target was, and in the third month one significant move in the market – well traded, with a good decision process enabled by his psychobiology – led to him exceeding his monthly target.

Practice: The Relaxing Sigh

This is a very quick and simple practice that you can use as you start to notice stress reactivity, or when you anticipate it. You can also use it throughout the day, taking 3 to 6 relaxing sighs, which will help to lower your stress reactivity. Triggers to practise could be arriving at your desk each time, or following a losing trade, or periodically on the hour as appropriate:

- Inhale through your nose and exhale through your mouth, making a quiet, relaxing sigh as you exhale.
- Take long, slow, gentle breaths that raise and lower your abdomen as you inhale and exhale.
- Focus on the sound and feeling of the breath.

Seven Ways to Turn Towards Difficulty

How any given trader approaches any given situation will be very individualistic. However, the research from psychology, neuroscience and mindfulness shows that there are core principles and strategies that traders can adopt of benefit to them in navigating such periods as successfully as possible – reducing their impact during the episodes and ensuring a quicker recovery and return to performance. Turning towards difficulty, whilst counterintuitive, is – as we have explored in this chapter – a potentially very effective approach for dealing with losses, periods of drawdown, changes in markets, institutional changes and challenges, and the plethora of events outside trading that can also create feelings of stress and contribute to exhaustion.

Below is a summary of some key approaches from this chapter, providing you with 7 ways in which – either individually or as a collective approach – you can turn towards difficulty:

1 Practise regular mindfulness training to provide you with the neurological and physiological changes that reduce your stress reactivity and bolster your stress capacity.
2 Use your "stress barometer" to monitor your physical feelings of stress throughout the day.
3 When you notice feelings of stress or exhaustion in the moment, turn towards them: *"What thoughts are there?" "What feelings are there?" "What bodily sensations are there?"*
4 When faced with stressful events, consider how you perceive them. Could you see this situation in a more useful way?
5 Hunt for the good stuff!
6 Use the breathing space, or relaxing sigh, or even 1-minute mindfulness to manage feelings of stress and exhaustion as required.
7 Focus on taking skillful and effective action – enjoyment, mastery, mindfulness.

10

The Mindful Trader and Investor

The Mindful Trader and Investor

Remember earlier in the book when I told you about the US Military's special forces soldiers who were a part of the once secret "Ultimate Warrior" training programme (also known as Jedi warriors) – designed to equip them with the skills to succeed on missions that no other teams had ever succeeded on before. A large part of this training focused on martial arts and meditation, including a 30-day silent retreat that was called "*The Encampment*". Those soldiers went on to become the most outstanding team in the NATO military games. We have seen in this book how, over 20 years later, the US Marines are utilising the same mind technology for success on the battlefield.

On the sports field, athletes and teams are tapping into the power of meditation in order to equip them with the mind fitness required to excel. Rapid response emergency services, the police, surgeons and pilots are all beginning to utilise mindfulness and meditation-based techniques to enhance their performance.

The aim of *TraderMind* has been to help you enhance your trading decisions, be able to respond more effectively to market events, develop the resilience to be able to cope with the outcomes of your trading decisions and the inherent pressures and stresses that trading the markets brings. Its focus has been to maximise your returns from the market by strengthening your psychology through developing a greater level of mindful awareness and attention.

Throughout the course of the book you have been introduced to the benefits of becoming a mindful or "mind fit" trader, including the effects of developing attention, emotion regulation, impulse control, integrating mind and body and enhancing self-discipline. By training your attention and awareness, working with your thoughts, embracing emotions, becoming more tuned into your feelings whilst keeping a focus on effective action, you create a greater opportunity for being able to read, respond to and trade the market more effectively.

The key to developing your mind fitness is, as you have discovered, through practice – just as physical fitness is acquired through training. The aim of this chapter is to help you develop ways of integrating mind fitness practice into your day, making it a key feature of your trading in much the same way as you might spend time researching, analysing and preparing.

Developing Mindfulness – Mind Fitness Practice

There are many ways in which you can sustain your mindfulness practice, and they fall under two key headings: formal and informal.

Formal mind fitness practice would include taking time to conduct, for example, a sitting breathing practice, the mindfulness of breath and body practice or the body scan, or perhaps some mindful movement. Much of the research into the benefits of mindfulness training demonstrates a clear link between the outcomes achieved and the amount of time spent practising.

Informal practice might include taking a mindful walk, eating or drinking mindfully, performing an automatic behaviour like brushing your teeth in a more mindful way, taking some time to conduct the 1-minute mindfulness or 3-minute breathing space practice throughout the day. Or just simply checking in with the breath and body every now and again.

In my experience it is a combination of both informal and formal practice that seems to be the most effective, with each feeding off the other in a virtuous circle. Even more so perhaps is the adoption of mindfulness as an approach, as a way of trading and investing, as a way of life, as a way of being.

Mindfulness for me is not just about doing my daily practice... it is more than that. It is a way of being. It is perhaps as much philosophical as psychological. For me just keeping a focus on where my attention is has been very powerful, alongside everything else.

A trader client

Yoga teachers often say that the most difficult move in yoga is the move onto your mat. Remember, being mindful is not difficult – it is remembering to be mindful that is difficult. You will need to make a conscious and committed effort towards developing your mind fitness if you wish to achieve the full benefits. One way of doing this is to find a strong and compelling reason to keep practising.

What is really important to you about your trading, and how might becoming more mindful and mindfulness practice help with that?

It is perfectly natural at some stage to relapse, to do less, or stop doing your practice all together. It is useful to have an awareness of this from the beginning and to have a relapse plan in place. What I mean by this is to have a mindset such that if you do relapse, then you can recognise this, refocus and return to practice. Relapse is not a sign of failure. There are many perfectly good reasons why your practice may have stopped. The goal is to start it again as soon as you can. Reminding yourself of your motivations for practising can be a useful strategy following a relapse. Also, perhaps start small again with a 1-minute practice or a 3-minute breathing space, or 5 minutes of mindfulness of the breath to get yourself moving again.

It is also important to consider which practices and approaches you will use going forward in designing your own mindfulness programme. You do not need to have a formalised "training plan" and you can, in fact, be extremely flexible in the practices that you do from day to day and week to week. It might be that a particular situation or set of events determines which is most useful. Perhaps a period of losing trades would be met with the *Turning Towards Difficulty* practise, or you may wish to develop your mind/body connection with the *Body Scan*.

10 Ways to Incorporate Mind Fitness into Your Trading Day

Here is a list of suggested ways in which you can begin to incorporate mindfulness into your trading day. Naturally, not all of them will be appropriate for all people. However, it should give you some ideas and you can then explore and adapt it as relevant for your own personal trading and lifestyle circumstances.

1 Take between 5 and 20 minutes in the morning to conduct a mindfulness practice of your choice. Jon Kabat-Zinn, in a presentation at Google, talked about the power of just 5 minutes of mindfulness at the start of the day. Beginning the day with a mindfulness practice can help you carry that mental state into and through the trading day.

2 On your commute take a minute to pay attention to your breathing; this can be done when you get into the car in the morning if you drive to work, or at a red light; it can also be done on the train or tube if that is your method of travelling. If you walk to work, incorporate a mindful walk within it.

3   When you arrive at work and get to your desk, before you get into the automatic routine of turning your screens on, reading news, looking at levels and getting into the throws of the markets, take a couple of moments to just sit and notice any bodily sensations, consciously letting go of any excess tension, focus on the feeling of contact with your chair or the floor.

4   During the day, if you have a chance to take a break, try taking a short mindful walk or have a *breathing break* and conduct the 1-minute mindfulness practice.

5   When you take lunch, if appropriate and possible, take some time away from your desk to refresh and change your environment; eat slowly and mindfully.

6   Throughout the day, perhaps every hour (you could set a quiet alarm on your phone or watch) take a minute or two to pay attention to your breathing, bringing your focus into the present.

7   Use the 3-minute breathing space when you feel stressed, angry, frustrated, anxious or any other powerful emotion. This will help you to manage your thoughts and emotions and put you into a better position from which to make a decision.

8   If you have the time, incorporate some mindful exercise into your day. Do whatever form of exercise you prefer, but perform it with a mindful and curious attitude, bringing an awareness to your body, noticing any sensations as they unfold.

9   At the end of the day, turn off your screens, tidy your desk and then just sit for a moment and reflect on the day. Bring your attention to your breath and body, consciously letting go of any tension that is present.

10   Use your commute home as a chance to transition from work to home. Walk mindfully, conduct a short mind fitness practice or simply sit and relax.

Take some time to think about how you can best build mind fitness training into your day, when and where it will be most effective for you to practise, and when you will be able to be most consistent with it.

Looking Back

Take a few minutes now to review your experience of reading this book. Take your mind back to the beginning when you started the Introduction, through the exercises and practices that you have completed, and reflect on your answers to the questions below.

- What did you come for?
- What were your expectations?
- What did you want/hope for?
- What did you get from reading the book?
- What have you learnt?
- What have you noticed that is different?
- What are the biggest obstacles towards carrying on?
- What might help you?

Looking Forward

It is my wish that reading *TraderMind* has just been the beginning of your own commitment to mindfulness training. Beyond *TraderMind* lies the opportunity to develop your mindfulness through the multitude of research, reading and recordings available and via both live and online training programmes. If you have not yet completed the *8-Week TraderMind Training Programme* at the back of the book, then that would be an excellent next step.

If I can be of any help whatsoever in the continuing development of your mind fitness, then please get in touch.

TraderMind: Mindfulness-Based Trading and Investing Training Programme

Overview

This is a framework for an 8-week programme of mindfulness training designed to help you incorporate the key themes, approaches, practices and strategies from this book into a real-world experience (the only way it can make any difference to your trading decisions and performance).

The programme starts off with a self-assessment exercise, including taking the *Mindful Attention and Awareness Scale* to give you a benchmark to measure progress against at the end of the programme.

Following the initial self-assessment, each week is explained in terms of the theme for the week, an overview of what you are working on and developing and its benefits, and then a reference to the practices and exercises that you will be required to complete and their relative frequency and duration.

Warning! This 8-week programme requires a high level of commitment to complete.

Mindful Attention and Awareness Scale

(*Also available to take online at www.highperformanceglobal.com/MAAS.*)

Please answer according to what really reflects your experience rather than what you think your experience should be:

1 = almost always
2 = very frequently
3 = somewhat frequently
4 = somewhat infrequently
5 = very infrequently
6 = almost never.

---

1   I could be experiencing some emotion and not be conscious of it until some time later.
2   I break or spill things because of carelessness, not paying attention or thinking of something else.
3   I find it difficult to stay focused on what's happening in the present.
4   I tend to walk quickly to get where I'm going without paying attention to what I experience along the way.
5   I tend not to notice feelings of physical tension or discomfort until they really grab my attention.
6   I forget a person's name almost as soon as I've been told it for the first time.
7   It seems I am "running on automatic" without much awareness of what I'm doing.
8   I rush through activities without being really attentive to them.
9   I get so focused on the goal I want to achieve that I lose touch with what I am doing right now to get there.
10 I do jobs or tasks automatically, without being aware of what I'm doing.
11 I find myself listening to someone with one ear, doing something else at the same time.
12 I drive places on "automatic pilot" and then wonder why I went there.
13 I find myself preoccupied with the future or the past.
14 I find myself doing things without paying attention.
15 I snack without being aware that I'm eating.

Source: Brown, K.W. and Ryan, R.M. (2003) The benefits of being present: Mindfulness and its role in psychological well-being. *Journal of Personality and Social Psychology,* **84**(4), 822–884.

Week 1 – Attention, Awareness and Automatic Pilot

- Read Chapter 3 and complete the appropriate exercises.
- Complete the *Mindfulness of Breathing* practice at least 5 times this week.
- At several times during the day, stop and simply focus your attention on your breath, for a minute – a *mindful minute*.
- *Habit releaser:* Choose a routine activity and make a deliberate effort to bring moment-to-moment awareness to it. This could be anything from making and drinking a cup of tea or coffee to brushing your teeth, having a shower, walking to work. Make sure that you are at the point of knowing what you are doing as you are doing it.
- Complete the practice form on page 196.

Week 2 – Thinking About Thinking

- Read Chapter 4 and complete the appropriate exercises.
- Complete the *Mindfulness of Sounds and Thoughts* practice at least 5 times this week.
- Check in during the day, taking time to notice your thinking as thoughts, mental events; watch them come and go without feeling that you have to hook on to them or follow them.
- Keep a thoughts diary. At the end of the day, write down key thoughts about the trading day that come to mind. Writing your thoughts down helps you to see them in a different way. The pause between having a thought and writing it down can give you a moment to reflect on its meaning.
- *Habit releaser:* Choose a different routine activity to bring full moment-to-moment awareness to.
- Complete the practice form.

Week 3 – Embracing Emotions

- Read Chapter 5 and complete the appropriate exercises.
- Complete the *Mindfulness of Body and Breath* practice at least 5 times this week.

- Check in during the day, taking time to notice your emotions. Notice them as emotions, "*I am feeling the emotion of...*"
- *Habit releaser:* Change the chair you sit in to watch television at home.
- Complete the practice form.

Week 4 – Managing Urges and Impulses

- Read Chapter 6 and complete the appropriate exercises.
- Complete any of the mindfulness practices from weeks 1 to 3 (your choice, and can be a combination) so you practise at least 5 times this week.
- As you become aware of any "urges" this week, practise your urge surfing technique.
- *Habit releaser:* Go for at least one 15-minute or longer walk this week; walk slowly and mindfully, take a look around, open up your senses.
- Complete the practice form.
- Take some time to reflect at the end of this week on the following questions:

What am I learning through this process?
What have I noticed so far?
What do I need to do over the next 4 weeks to get the most from this course?

Week 5 – Trading With the Body in Mind

- Read Chapter 7 and complete the appropriate exercises.
- Complete the *Body Scan* practice at least 5 times this week.
- Bring a mindful and curious attention to bodily sensations, intuitions and gut feelings during this week.
- Focus on nurturing your body with good habits of sleep, exercise, nutrition and rest.
- *Habit releaser:* Aim to have at least one mindful meal per day this week, or choose a different way to exercise.
- Complete the practice form.

Week 6 – Habits, Behaviour and Action

- Read Chapter 8 and complete the appropriate exercises.
- Complete any of the mindfulness practices, in any combination, so you practise at least 5 times this week.
- Focus on performing behaviours that will be most effective in your trading decision making and performance. Build a really strong performance funnel. What will those behaviours be? Write them down. Make yourself accountable.
- Bring an awareness to your habitual tendencies and actions, patterns of thinking and feeling.
- *Habit releaser:* Start a new habit this week. Think of an action or behaviour that would really benefit your trading performance and start it this week.
- Complete the practice form.

Week 7 – Turning Towards Difficulty

- Read Chapter 9 and complete the appropriate exercises.
- Complete any of the mindfulness practices from weeks 1 to 5 (your choice, and can be a combination) so you practise at least 5 times this week.
- Practise the *3-Minute Breathing Space* at least 3 times per day. Do this as you feel it is required, or connect it to regular activities you do or places you go (e.g., on waking up/ before going to bed; on sitting at your desk first thing in the morning/before leaving last thing at night; at lunchtime; on your commute; before a data release; after exiting a losing trade).
- Notice the times when you experience difficulty within your trading. Notice your reactions to these situations. Think about some strategies from the book that you can use to help you manage these situations.
- *Habit releaser:* Think about an activity that you really enjoy doing, maybe something that you did more of in the past when perhaps life was less busy. Find time this week to revisit one of those activities.
- Complete the practice form.

Practice Record

Day/Date/Time	Practice	Comments

Week 8 – The Mindful Trader

- Read Chapter 10 and complete the appropriate exercises.
- From all of the different forms of "formal" mind fitness practice that you have experienced from the book and over the last 7 weeks, start to develop for yourself a regular mindfulness practice that you can continue beyond week 8.
- *Habit releaser:* Focus on building the habit of mindfulness, creating your own mind fitness programme going forward.
- Complete the practice form.

Review

Firstly, if you have completed the full 8-week programme then a big "well done" because it takes a significant investment of time, energy and commitment to do so. I am sure that, as a result, you have already noticed some changes in your trading experience and now is a great time to capture these. It would also be useful to retake the *Mindful Attention and Awareness Scale* and see what you notice; perhaps record your key observations below.

- What have you got out of completing the 8-week *TraderMind* programme?

- What have you learnt?

- What differences have you noticed in your trading and in yourself?

- How will you continue your mind fitness practice? What obstacles are there? How can you overcome them?

What Next?

Having read the book and completed the 8-week training programme, the big question is: "*What next?*" Going forward I would encourage you to read more on the topic of mindfulness to deepen your understanding; you could also consider attending a live mindfulness training course near to your location. The real aim, though, is to integrate mindfulness into your everyday trading approach, to make it a part of your lifestyle and to continue your practice well into the future.

You can find out more about mindfulness training for traders at www.performanceedgeconsulting.co.uk/tradermind

References

Introduction

(1) Smith, A. (1759). *The Theory of Moral Sentiments*. Printed for A. Millar, London.

(2) Williams, N. (2012). FX traders seek coaching in battle for dominance. Available at: uk.reuters.com/article/2012/09/30/uk-markets-forex-coaches-idUKBRE88T03G20120930.

(3) Khan, J. (2014). Finding your inner trader. *Bloomberg Markets Magazine*, April.

(4) Saft, J. (2013). Meditation and the art of investment. Available at: blogs.reuters.com/james-saft/2013/04/17/meditation-and-the-art-of-investment/.

(5) Burton, K. and Effinger, A. (2014). How to make a killing on Wall Street, start meditating. Available at: www.bloomberg.com/news/2014-05-28/to-make-killing-on-wall-street-start-meditating.html.

Chapter One

(1) Kabat-Zinn, J. (2004). *Full Catastrophe Living: How to Cope with Stress, Pain and Illness Using Mindfulness Meditation*. Piatkus Books, London.

(2) Chaskalson, M. (2011). *The Mindful Workplace: Developing Resilient Individuals and Resonant Organisations with MBSR*. Wiley-Blackwell, Oxford.

(3) Williams, M. and Penman, D. (2011). *Mindfulness: A Practical Guide to Finding Peace in a Frantic World*. Piatkus Books, London.

(4) Ruiz, F.J. and Luciano, C. (2012). Improving international-level chess players' performance with an acceptance-based protocol: Preliminary findings. *Psychological Record*, **62**(3), 447–461.

(5) Crocker, P.R.E., Alderman, R.B. and Smith, F.M.R. (1988). Cognitive-affective stress management training with high performance youth volleyball players: Effects on affect, cognition, and performance. *Journal of Sport & Exercise Psychology*, **10**(4), 448–460.

(6) Gardner, F.L. and Moore, Z.E. (2007). *The Psychology of Enhancing Human Performance: The Mindfulness–Acceptance–Commitment (MAC) Approach*. Springer, New York, p. 28.

(7) Douglas, M. (2000). *Trading in the Zone: Master the Market with Confidence, Discipline and a Winning Attitude*. Prentice-Hall, Englewood Cliffs, NJ.

(8) www.wisdomatwork.com/WisdomAtWork/JEDIWARRIOR.html.

(9) www.washingtontimes.com/news/2012/dec/5/marines-expanding-use-of-meditation-training/?page=all.

(10) www.amishi.com/lab/wp-content/uploads/jha_stanley_etal_emotion_2010.pdf.

(11) Hölzel, B.K., Carmody, J., Vangel, M. *et al.* (2011). Mindfulness practice leads to increases in regional brain gray matter density. *Psychiatry Research: Neuroimaging*, **191**(1), 36–43.

(12) www.mentalhealth.org.uk/publications/be-mindful-report/.

(13) Langer, E. and Beard, A. (2014). Mindfulness in the age of complexity. *Harvard Business Review*, **March**, 68–73.

(14) van Overveld, M., Mehta, P., Smidts, A., Figner, B. and Lins, J. (2012). Paying attention to emotions pays off: Emotion regulation training improves financial decision-making. Paper presented at NeuroPsychoEconomics Conference, Rotterdam, The Netherlands, 14–15 June.

(15) Hafenback, A.C., Kinias, Z. and Barsade, S.G. (2013). Debiasing the mind through meditation: Mindfulness and the sunk-cost bias. Available at: www.psychologicalscience

.org/index.php/news/releases/mindfulness-meditation-may-improve-decision-making.html.

(16) Criswell, C. and Martin, A. (2007). 10 Trends – A study of senior executive views on the future. Centre for Creative Leadership Research White Paper.

(17) www.upenn.edu/pennnews/news/building-fit-minds-under-stress-penn-neuroscientists-examine-protective-effects-mindfulness-tra.

Chapter Two

(1) Brown, K.W. and Ryan, R.M. (2003). The benefits of being present: Mindfulness and its role in psychological well-being. *Journal of Personality and Social Psychology*, **84**(4), 822–848.

(2) Gonzalez, M. and Byron, G. (2010). *The Mindful Investor*. Wiley, Chichester, pp. 12–13.

(3) Doidge, N. (2007). *The Brain That Changes Itself: Stories of Personal Triumph From The Frontiers of Brain Science*. Penguin, Harmondsworth.

(4) *MBSR Course Manual*.

(5) Granath, J., Ingvarsson, S., von Thiele, U. and Lundberg, U. (2006). Stress management: A randomized study of cognitive behavioural therapy and yoga. *Cognitive Behaviour Therapy*, **35**(1), 3–10.

(6) Ferris, T. (2011). *The Four Hour Body*. Vermilion, London.

(7) uonews.uoregon.edu/archive/news-release/2012/6/chinese-meditation-ibmt-prompts-double-positive-punch-brain-white-matter.

(8) Tang, Y.-Y., Lu, Q., Geng, X., Stein, E.A., Yang, Y. and Posner, M.I. (2010). Short-term meditation induces white matter changes in the anterior cingulate. *Proceedings of the National Academy of Sciences*, **107**(35), 15,649–15,652.

(9) oro.open.ac.uk/34544/1/Final%20report%20-%20publishable%20format.pdf.

(10) Puddicombe, A. (2011). *Headspace: Ten Minutes a Day Can Make All The Difference*. Hodder and Stoughton, London.

(11) Davidson, R.J., Kabat-Zinn, J., Schumacher, J. *et al.* (2003). Alterations in brain and immune function produced by mindfulness meditation. *Psychosomatic Medicine*, **65**(4), 564–570.

(12) Anders Ericsson, K. (ed.) (1996). *The Road to Excellence: The Acquisition of Expert Performance in the Arts, Sciences, Sports and Games*. Lawrence Erlbaum Associates, Mahwah, NJ.

(13) www.simplypsychology.org/learning-kolb.html.

(14) Shapiro, S., Carlson, L., Astin, J. and Freedman, B. (2006). Mechanisms of mindfulness. *Journal of Clinical Psychology*, **62**(3), 373–386.

Chapter Three

(1) Bradberry, T. (2009). *Self Awareness – The Hidden Driver of Success and Satisfaction*. Perigee Trade, New York.

(2) Rock, D. (2009). *Your Brain At Work: Strategies For Overcoming Distraction, Regaining Focus and Working Smarter All Day Long*. Harper Collins, London.

(3) Carlson, E.N. (2013). Overcoming the barriers to self-knowledge: Mindfulness as a path to seeing yourself as you really are. *Perspectives on Psychological Science*, **8**(2), 173–186.

(4) Van Tharp, K. (2011). *Super Trader: Make Consistent Profits In Good and Bad Markets*. McGraw-Hill, New York.

(5) Whitmore, J. (2002). *Coaching for Performance*. Nicholas Brealey Publishing, London.

(6) Chaskalson, M. (2011). *The Mindful Workplace: Developing Resilient Individuals and Resonant Organisations with MBSR*. Wiley-Blackwell, Oxford.

(7) Tang, Y.-Y., Lu, Q., Geng, X., Stein, E.A., Yang, Y. and Posner, M.I. (2010). Short-Term Meditation Induces White Matter Changes in the Anterior Cingulate. *Proceedings of the National Academy of Sciences*, **107**(35), 15,649–15,652.

(8) Endsley, M. (1997). Situational awareness model: Toward a theory of situation awareness in dynamic systems. *Human Factors*, **37**(1), 32–64.

(9) Mallaby, S. (2010). *More Money Than God: Hedge Funds and the Making of a New Elite*. Penguin, Harmondsworth.

(10) Krasner, M.S., Epstein, R.M., Beckman, H. *et al.* (2009). Association of an educational program in mindful communication with burnout, empathy, and attitudes among primary care physicians. *JAMA*, **302**(12), 1284–1293.

(11) Wallace, B.A. (2006). *The Attention Revolution: Unlocking The Power of The Focused Mind.* Wisdom Publications, Somerville, MA.

(12) MacLean, K.A., Ferrer, E., Aichele, S.R. *et al.* (2010). Intensive meditation training improves perceptual discrimination and sustained attention. *Psychological Science*, **21**(6), 829–839.

(13) Hallowell, E.M. (2007). Overloaded circuits: Why smart people underperform. *Harvard Business Review: On Point*, Winter.

(14) Moffitt, T., Arseneault, L., Belsky, D. *et al.* (2011). From the cover: A gradient of childhood self-control predicts health, wealth, and public safety. *Proceedings of the National Academy of Sciences*, **108**(7), 2693–2698.

(15) Mischel, W., Shoda, Y. and Peake, P.K. (1988). The nature of adolescent competencies predicted by preschool delay of gratification. *Journal of Personality and Social Psychology*, **54**(4), 687–696.

Chapter Four

(1) Van Tharp, K. (2006). *Trade Your Way to Financial Freedom.* McGraw-Hill, New York.

(2) Wegner, D.M., Schneider, D.J., Carter, S. and White, T. (1987). Paradoxical effects of thought suppression. *Journal of Personality and Social Psychology*, **53**, 5–13; also written about in his book *White Bears and Other Unwanted Thoughts*, published by Guilford Press in 1992.

(3) Garland, E.L., Gaylord, S.A. and Fredickson, B.L. (2011). Positive reappraisal mediates the stress-reductive effects of mindfulness: An upward spiral process. *Mindfulness*, **2**, 59–67.

(4) Williams, M. and Penman, D. (2011). *Mindfulness: A Practical Guide to Finding Peace in a Frantic World.* Piatkus Books, London.

(5) Bryant, R.A., Sutherland, K. and Guthrie, R.M. (2007). Impaired specific autobiographical memory as a risk factor for posttraumatic stress after trauma. *Journal of Abnormal Psychology*, **116**, 837–841.

(6) Kleim, B. and Ehlers, A. (2008). Reduced autobiographical memory specificity predicts depression and posttraumatic stress disorder after recent trauma. *Journal of Consulting and Clinical Psychology*, **76**(2), 231–242.

(7) Hayes, S.C., Strosahl, K.D. and Wilson, K.G. (2012). *Acceptance and Commitment Therapy: The Process and Practice of Mindful Change*. Guilford Press, New York.

Chapter Five

(1) Wang, S. (2010). *The Neuroscience of Everyday Life*. The Great Courses.

(2) Damasio, A. (2006). *Descartes' Error*. Vintage, London.

(3) Slovic, P., Finucane, M.L., Peters, E. and MacGregor, D.D. (2002). Risk as analysis and risk as feelings: Some thoughts about affect, reason, risk and rationality. *Risk Analysis*, **24**(2), 311–322.

(4) Seo, M.-G. and Barrett, L.F. (2007). Being emotional during decision making – good or bad? An empirical investigation. *PubMed Central*, **50**(4), 923–940.

(5) Dr Kevin Oschner, Director of Columbia University's Social Cognitive Neuroscience Laboratory in the USA, interviewed in Andrew Steadman's book *Applying Neuroscience to Enhance Tactical Leader Cognitive Performance in Combat*. BiblioScholar, 2012.

(6) Peffer, G. and Fenton-O'Creevy, M. (2012). *xDelia Final Report: Emotion-Centred Financial Decision Making and Learning*. Open University, CIMNE, Milton Keynes.

(7) Bradberry, T. and Greaves, J. (2009). *Emotional Intelligence 2.0*. TalentSmart, San Diego, CA.

(8) Williams, M. and Penman, D. (2011). *Mindfulness: A Practical Guide to Finding Peace in a Frantic World*. Piatkus Books, London.

(9) Mark Cook, interviewed in Jack Schwager's book *Stock Market Wizards*. Harper Business, 2003.

(10) Ed Seykota, www.seykota.com/tribe.
(11) Lieberman, M.D., Eisenberger, N.I., Crockett, M.J., Tom, S.J., Pfeifer, J.H. and Way, B.M. (2007). Putting feelings into words: Affect labelling disrupts amygdala activity in response to affective stimuli. *Psychological Science*, **18**(5), 421–428.
(12) www.nytimes.com/roomfordebate/2012/11/25/will-diaries-be-published-in-2050/diaries-a-healthy-choice.

Chapter Six

(1) Warren Buffett quote. Available at: en.wikiquote.org/wiki/Warren_Buffett.
(2) Marlatt, G.A. and Donovan, D.M. (2005). *Relapse Prevention: Maintenance Strategies in the Treatment of Addictive Behaviours*. Guilford Press, New York.

Chapter Seven

(1) Bechara, A., Damasio, H., Tranel, D. and Damasio, A.R. (2005). The Iowa Gambling Task and the somatic marker hypothesis: Some questions and answers. *Trends in Cognitive Sciences*, **9**(4), 159–162.
(2) Lehrer, J. (2009). *How We Decide*. Houghton Mifflin Harcourt, Boston, MA.
(3) Azzopardi, P.V. (2010). *Behavioural Technical Analysis: An Introduction to Behavioural Finance and its Role in Technical Analysis*. Harriman House, Hampshire.
(4) Peterson, R. (2007). *Inside the Investor's Brain*. Wiley Trading, Chichester.
(5) Finucane, M.L., Alhakami, A., Slovic, P. and Johnson, S.M. (2000). The affect heuristic in judgements of risks and benefits. *Journal of Behavioural Decision Making*, **13**, 1–17.
(6) Gigerenzer, G. (2014). *Risk Savvy: How to Make Good Decisions*. Allen Lane, Harmondsworth.
(7) Klein, G. (2007). *The Power of Intuition: How to Use Your Gut Feelings to Make Better Decisions at Work*. Crown Business, New York.
(8) Salk, J. (1983). *Anatomy of Reality: Merging of Intuition and Reason*. Columbia University Press, New York.

(9) Faith, C. (2009). *Trading From the Gut: How to Use Right Brain Instinct and Left Brain Smarts to Become a Master Trader.* FT Press, London.

(10) Shull, D. (2011). *Market Mind Games: A Radical Psychology of Investing, Trading and Risk.* McGraw-Hill, New York.

(11) John Coates. Available at: smartblogs.com/finance/2013/03/12/the-neuroscience-of-risk/.

(12) Danzigera, S., Levavb, J. and Avnaim-Pesso, L. (2011). Extraneous factors in judicial decisions. *Proceedings of the National Academy of Sciences USA,* **108**(17), 6889–6892.

(13) Scholey, A.B., Harper, S. and Kennedy, D.O. (2001). Cognitive demand and blood glucose. *Physiology & Behavior,* **73**, 585–592.

(14) Kahneman, D. (2012). *Thinking Fast and Slow.* Penguin, Harmondsworth.

(15) Baumeister, R. (2012). *Willpower: Rediscovering Our Greatest Strength.* Allen Lane, Harmondsworth.

(16) corporate.dukemedicine.org/news_and_publications/news_office/news/sleep-deprived-people-make-risky-decisions-based-on-too-much-optimism.

(17) National Sleep Foundation (2013) *National Sleep Foundation 2013 International Bedroom Poll First to Explore Sleep Differences among Six Countries.* http://sleepfoundation.org/media-center/press-release/national-sleep-foundation-2013-international-bedroom-poll

(18) Kilgore, W.D.S. (2010). Asleep at the trigger: War fighter judgement and decision making during prolonged wakefulness. In Bartone, P.T. (ed.), *The 71F Advantage. Applying Army Research Psychology for Health and Performance Gains.* Military Bookshop, Uckfield, pp. 59–67.

(19) Ong, J.C., Shapiro, S.L. and Manber, R. (2008). Combining mindfulness meditation with cognitive-behavior therapy for insomnia: A treatment development study. *Behavior Therapy,* **39**(2), 171–182; Ong, J.C., Shapiro, S.L. and Manber, R. (2009). Mindfulness meditation and cognitive behavioral therapy for insomnia: A naturalistic 12-month follow-up. *EXPLORE: The Journal of Science and Healing,* **5**(1), 30–36.

(20) Jacobs, G., Benson, H. and Friedman, R. (1996). Perceived benefits in a behavioral-medicine insomnia program: A clinical report. *The American Journal of Medicine*, **100**(2), 212–216.

(21) Loehr, J. (1997). *Stress for Success: The Proven Program for Transforming Stress into Positive Energy at Work*. Random House, London.

(22) Rossi, E. (1991). *The 20 Minute Break: Reduce Stress, Maximise Performance, Improve Health and Emotional Well Being Using The New Science of Ultradian Rhythms*. Zeig, Ticker & Co., Phoenix, AZ.

Chapter Eight

(1) Gardner, F.L. and Moore, Z.E. (2007). *The Psychology of Enhancing Human Performance: The Mindfulness–Acceptance–Commitment (MAC) Approach*. Springer, New York.

(2) *Any Given Sunday*, directed by Oliver Stone, 1999.

(3) Syed, M. (2013). Shock exclusive: Top footballer refuses bribe. *The Times*, 10th December. Available at: www.thetimes .co.uk/tto/opinion/columnists/article3944344.ece.

Chapter Nine

(1) Yerkes–Dodson curve developed by psychologists Robert M. Yerkes and John Dillingham Dodson in 1908.

(2) Coates, J. (2012). *The Hour Between Dog and Wolf: Risk Taking, Gut Feelings and the Biology of Boom and Bust*. Fourth Estate, London.

(3) Maddi, S. and Kobasa, S. (1984). *The Hardy Executive: Health Under Stress*. Irwin Professional Publishing, Burr Ridge, IL.

(4) Williams, M. and Penman, D. (2011). *Mindfulness: A Practical Guide to Finding Peace in a Frantic World*. Piatkus Books, London.

(5) Agnew, H. (2014). Mindfulness gives stressed out bankers something to think about. FT.com. Available at: www.ft.com/cms/s/0/331b85d0-d20d-11e3-8b5b-00144feabdc0.html#axzz34u22zpsA.

(6) The Huffington Post (2013). Mindfulness Meditation Could Lower Levels of Cortisol, The Stress Hormone. Available at www.huffingtonpost.com/2013/03/31/mindfulness-meditation-cortisol-stress-levels_n_2965197.html.

(7) Goldin, P.R. and Gross, J.J. (2010). Effects of mindfulness-based stress reduction (MBSR) on emotion regulation in social anxiety disorder. *Emotion*, **10**(1), 83–91.

(8) Hölzel, B.K., Carmody, J., Evans, K.C. *et al.* (2009). Stress reduction correlates with structural changes in the amygdala. *Social Cognitive and Affective Neuroscience*, **5**, 11–17.

(9) Friedman, R.S. and Forster, J. (2001). The effects of promotion and prevention cues on creativity. *Journal of Personality and Social Psychology*, **81**(6), 1001–1013.

(10) Tomarken, A.J., Davidson, R.J., Wheeler, R.E. and Doss, R.C. (1992). Individual differences in anterior brain asymmetry and fundamental dimensions of emotion. *Journal of Personality and Social Psychology*, **62**(4), 676–687.

(11) Davidson, R.J., Kabat-Zinn, J., Schumacher, J. *et al.* (2003). Alterations in brain and immune function produced by mindfulness meditation. *Psychosomatic Medicine*, **65**, 564–570.

(12) Lo, A.W. and Repin, D.V. (2002). The psychophysiology of real-time financial risk processing. *Journal of Cognitive Neuroscience*, **14**(3), 323–339.

(13) Marie Åsberg, Mindfulness Exhaustion Funnel, Karolinska Institute, Stockholm.

(14) Mackenzie, C.S., Poulin, P.A. and Seidman-Carlson, R. (2006). A brief mindfulness-based stress reduction intervention for nurses and nurse aides. *PubMed, Applied Nursing Research*, **19**(2), 105–109.

(15) Alexander, C.N., Swanson, G.C., Rainforth, M.V. *et al.* (1993). Effects of the transcendental meditation program on stress reduction, health and employee development: A prospective study in two occupational settings. *Anxiety, Stress and Coping International*, **6**, 245–262.

Index